Mohr, Marian M.

Working together

$7.25

DATE			

© THE BAKER & TAYLOR CO.

Working Together

Working Together

A Guide for Teacher-Researchers

Marian M. Mohr
Marion S. MacLean
Fairfax County (Virginia) Public Schools

National Council of Teachers of English
1111 Kenyon Road, Urbana, Illinois 61801

Book Design: Tom Kovacs for TGK Design

NCTE Stock Number 58234   60 / 44 937

Library of Congress Cataloging-in-Publication Data

Mohr, Marian M.
   Working together.

   Includes bibliographies.
   1. Action research in education.   2. Teachers.
3. Cooperation.   4. Group work in education.
I. MacLean, Marion S.   II. Title.
LB1028.24.M64   1987   371.1′0072   87-23956
ISBN 0-8141-5823-4

Contents

Introduction

In both elementary schools and high schools, teachers are isolated from one another, and the regimented quality of the school day perpetuates that isolation. In one day of teaching it is possible to have many intense emotional and intellectual exchanges with students, to experience in less than an hour a wider range of thought and emotion than people outside the profession can imagine, and yet at the end of the day to feel as if you have been separated from the world, solitary and lonely. Teaching is exhausting; a teacher responds to the needs of as many as 150 students a day—their need to learn and their need for emotional support. As a result, teachers may shun further human interaction in their professional lives. The isolation, the exhaustion, and the need to pull away conflict directly with a teacher's corresponding need for more contact with colleagues, both for friendly support and for professional discourse.

It takes remarkable effort, then, for teachers to work together, supporting one another and collectively improving their teaching. Teacher-researchers, however, go a step further. They assume the professional responsibility of documenting, analyzing, and writing about their work for other teachers. At present most teacher-researchers work in the evening after the school day with minimal support from their school systems. They add to their exhaustion by extending their day and their commitment to other teachers, and they do this in order to make their profession less exhausting and isolating for themselves and their colleagues.

Classroom research is an effort of great importance. The purposes of this book are to show how a teacher-researcher group works, to assist other groups in beginning, and to interest the educational community in supporting such groups. In response to requests from program directors and other teachers for guidelines and bibliographies on organizing teacher-researcher groups, we decided to write about what we had learned from our experience over the past several years in a teacher-researcher seminar. The first of these seminars,

1

led by Marian Mohr and supported by the Northern Virginia Writing Project at George Mason University, was offered in 1981–82. The seminar was repeated, and in 1984 Marion MacLean joined Mohr as coleader.

From the beginning, however, we—the authors—thought that the framework of a graduate course was not essential. We hoped that school systems would see the worth of classroom research studies conducted by teachers, recognizing these studies as contributions to educational research in general and also as support for the school systems' own curriculum and staff development planning. We hoped that released time would be provided and that collaborative research between teachers or with local colleges and universities would grow. We saw the idea of the teacher-researcher as a model for professional growth, recognition, and advancement that does not remove the teacher from the classroom.

In the meantime, however, we offered the course in order to provide interested teachers with some form of reward (course credit) for their efforts. Because we do not want this course viewed necessarily as a graduate course, we refer to the teacher-researchers as a *group* throughout this book. In fact, teachers did meet in support groups during the year before the first course and in the intervening year between the second and third seminars to develop and continue their interest in classroom research.

Although the course itself continues, a few school-based groups of teachers in our district have started to conduct classroom research outside the graduate course context with support from the school system. These groups are organized similarly to those described in this book, with the additional possibilities of daily contact among teachers and some free days for teachers to work on their studies. The work is related to their schools' and district's priorities, but their research questions are their own. At least one of the teachers in each of these groups has participated in the seminar.

We are pleased that other teacher-researcher groups are forming at various sites of the National Writing Project, using a variety of organizational formats, some based on the ideas presented here. The Bread Loaf School of English, the Alaska State Writing Consortium, and the teacher-researcher grants sponsored by the Research Foundation of the National Council of Teachers of English also support teacher-researcher work.

In this evolving context, we will describe what we consider the essential components of any teacher-researcher group. We trust that other group leaders will adapt and improve upon our work. The suggestions are as free of the restraints of a typical graduate course as possible, yet cull from the course what could work in other contexts. We think it is important to write about what we know now, as researchers making tentative attempts at analysis early in the data-gathering process. Knowledge about what happens or needs to happen in teacher-researcher groups is acquired at an early stage.

The group, as it has been organized, meets over the span of a year, and the participants develop their own research questions, plan their own methodology, analyze their own data, and write their own articles. As instructors of the group we function mostly as organizers and responders—roles that have led us to refer to ourselves as "leaders" instead of "instructors." Learning in the group comes from the interaction among its members, both leaders and participants.

Both of us, who are secondary school teachers in Fairfax County, Virginia, teach, conduct our own research, and lead the seminar of K–12 teachers from various northern Virginia school systems. Most of the other teachers in the group have participated in the Northern Virginia Writing Project Summer Institute or have taken the NVWP graduate course "Writing and Learning."

Because of our backgrounds, the teacher-researcher group we describe focuses on research in writing and language, not on educational research in general. Although several of the studies deal with the relationship between language and learning, rather than with learning to write, we have come to our interest in classroom research through our interest in learning more about how our students write.

We believe that the research of teachers need not be limited to studies of language use, however, and hope that the practices we describe will be of value to teachers in other disciplines. We have some basis for believing that the process can be used in many fields, since the group has included teachers of physics, biology, and psychology and since two teacher-researchers have done their research on adult learners. The groups currently forming in our school district represent many disciplines.

One other subject should be addressed before we begin: why we use the term *teacher-researcher*. This hyphenated name implies a contrast between traditional assumptions about educational research and assumptions about teachers. Outside the university, teachers are not usually researchers, and researchers are not usually teachers.

What teachers have to add to educational research is the sorely missed context of the classroom. Therefore, the most common kind of research teachers conduct is qualitative, hypothesis-raising, and descriptive. Teachers have been participant-observers, to use the ethnographic term, for years. Traditional educational research, based on the experimental, hypothesis-testing model with its limited variables, has not always served teachers well. We believe that teacher-researchers will choose to conduct many different kinds of research and, in collaboration with other teachers, will develop and extend their methodologies, seeing value in statistical studies as well as in case studies.

We reject the idea that classroom teachers are not qualified to be researchers or that their research results will fall short of professional standards. Teachers do not "pretend" to do research, and their research exhibits the same variety of form and content that exists in educational research in general.

As they begin to think of themselves as researchers, teachers are moved to redefine their roles as teachers. As their research becomes integrated into their teaching, their definition of teacher-researcher becomes *teacher*—a teacher who observes, questions, assists, analyzes, writes, and repeats these actions in a recursive process that includes sharing their results with their students and with other teachers.

Because our guide to this process is based on these assumptions about research and teachers, it, too, is divided and recursive. To make the description more manageable, we have separated it into four sections. The first includes the elements of the group's organization and the procedures that are crucial to its functioning. We have included in this section our personal choices for readings that have been helpful both to the leaders of the group and to the teacher-researchers. The second section describes the general process the group follows as it engages in research. The third looks at some of the issues and complexities of this research process, especially why it is difficult and yet very rewarding. The fourth presents a few teachers' final research reports from the publications compiled at the end of each year's work.

It should be noted here that we have edited minimally (for spelling and punctuation) the excerpts from teacher-researchers' logs and from student writings since they were not originally intended for publication.

Group Organization
and Procedures

"I really enjoyed getting the feedback on 'what do I have' when I read those student insights, and I found the discussion about owning learning to be crucial in helping me formulate a 'what does it mean' conjecture. I wish I had been ready then with 'what I'll do next . . .' "

Time and Timing

Research is time-consuming work that must be conducted in stages. The teacher-researcher group meets throughout the school year. During the first half of the year (September to mid-December), we focus on data collection. During the second half (mid-December through April), we work on data analysis and the writing of the final report. This timing also allows the teacher-researchers to take advantage of their teaching schedules, for even when they stop collecting data and concentrate on analyzing what they have, they are still working daily with students. It's only a matter of meeting the next day for another observation, interview, or follow-up questionnaire to check out what they think they are seeing. They don't have to worry about maintaining contact or reestablishing trust.

We arrange for the group to meet biweekly for three hours in the evening. Usually the whole group discusses articles during the first half of the session and divides into small groups for more intensive discussion during the second half, taking a short break for dinner or snacks and informal talk in between. (See Appendix A for a sample course outline and Appendix B for a sample course description.)

One of our concerns has been the extraordinary amount of time that these full-time teachers put into their research. Although the group agrees to meet from 4:00 to 7:00 p.m., people frequently stay longer to help each other. They call each other and the group leaders between meetings, hold additional meetings of their individual support groups (especially as the time nears for the final reports), and take personal leave from school to work on their articles. After the publication of the group's research reports at the end of the year, many continue to raise and investigate questions in their own classrooms. Some join the group for a second year; others pursue their research in graduate programs. The commitment of time and energy that begins with the first research experience seems to continue. It is demanding work, but work that teachers value enough to devote themselves to wholeheartedly.

The Research Log

At the group's first meeting, we ask teachers to write what they have noticed in their classrooms that makes them curious, something they would like to find out more about. As they write, they pinpoint the issues that have concerned them most. This initial writing is the first of many attempts they will make to formulate research questions. Their response becomes the first entry in their log, the initial field notes of their research.

Example 1: Initial Log Entries

(From the log of Pam Curtis, high school English teacher, 1981–82) 9/22/81

One thing I'd like to know is about parent involvement in the writing process. I have required my students to send papers through an adult (parent) editor for the past year, and I think it was of some benefit. I came up with the idea last Back-to-School Night and I'm not sure whether I see a benefit because I'm defending an idea I liked or whether the adult editor really contributes something worthwhile to the writing process.

How can I find out? What questions can I ask? How can I observe a parent responding to his or her offspring's paper? Go to the parent's house? Ask parents to come to school? Involve them in the classroom process?

Perhaps I'll find the whole requirement is counterproductive— so what?

I've already sent out and gotten back parent questionnaires about their own involvement with and attitudes toward writing. Could I do something with those other than just tabulate them and forget it?

(From the log of Alberta Grossman, teacher of learning-disabled high school students, 1981–82)
9/22/81

My husband says I-Search is a phony idea. I don't think so. What I want to know is—can I get students who can write adequately to write *more* adequately and/or to feel more competent when they are writing about information and ideas? (I suspect that information and ideas are not the same—that is, do not present the same writing problem.) Something happens to stop the words from coming out of the pen under certain circumstances for some people. Take me, for instance; back in college, I used to sit for hours unable to produce a single word—or I would get down a few nice phrases and nothing else. The problem is "nothing to say"—no thoughts about something because of no experience(?)—or what? This doesn't seem to be going too far. Is it better to keep writing—producing junk—than to produce nothing at all?

The first thoughts about the thinking/writing connections came from my own experience at [college]. But little glimmers of light have been shed on the problem since last summer in the writing project.

Fact one: Bernie Glaze [another teacher-researcher] told how well her students did in nonessay responses to social studies topics and how relatively poorly they did on essay test responses.
Question: Were her standards lower or different?
—Did good literary quality cover up lack of information or thought? (I, from my own experience, would say, "probably yes.")
—Or was it possible to accept "inferred" information/ideas in nonessay writing?

More glimmers of light from Peter Elbow—when ideas are conflicting or confusing, writing stops.

More from Bernie—I-Search better than research—papers more interesting, more coherent, more believable when students wrote about what they were interested in (knew about/already had questions about).

Research in reading shows that people who read actively (with a question) do better (learn more) than people who don't.

Britton says writing (good writing?) arises from the *expressive need* (?) (need to look that up) so having something to say or ask is paramount.

This is begging the question(?).

What about Lunsford's student who would always say, "I'll do it the easy way" and then start with an I-centered story?

According to Piaget (and Bruner and others), all learning begins as I-centered and *thing*-centered (concrete).

After this initial log writing and before the next meeting, we ask the teacher-researchers to observe some of their students as they write—simply to describe them as nonjudgmentally as possible. We talk about choosing a time when students are writing so that the teacher can look up and observe, then jot down what seems to be going on. We ask teachers to reread what they have written later and to write once more. This time they evaluate the observation, indicating any differences they notice about observing their classrooms in this way, any understandings that seem to have emerged from their rereading, and any feelings they experienced during the observation.

Example 2: Observations and Reflections from Teachers' Logs

(From the log of Veronica Brown, high school English teacher, 1982–83)

10/14/82: Period 3

The students are writing a timed essay. They have been allowed to use their reading logs, so many of them are flipping through their notes, pausing occasionally to ponder a point/idea. One minute lapses. Everyone is now writing. Pens are moving quickly across the page. They're hovering over their papers, intently pushing pens rapidly across their papers. One boy scratches his head, pauses, then begins to write again. One girl is turning pages, mouthing the words she is reading. She begins to write, moving her head very close to the paper. Everyone has at least one arm on the table, and many have both; their heads are resting on their arms. I remember that I was always told to sit up straight, with my back against the back of the chair, feet flat on the floor, and my left hand in my lap. I remember many spasmodic movements in elementary school, when I tried to get comfortable while sitting like a statue. This is a new day. Several students pause, their heads on their arms, or hands, concentrating. Then they begin to write again. One student keeps shaking his right leg as he frantically writes with his left hand. His right foot is propped against the table leg.

Interrupted: "How do you spell *con*?" I point to the dictionary. Student rushes over to get dictionary, frustration evident as he sighs loudly.

Interrupted again: "How do you spell *innocent?*" I write it on a scrap of paper. Student returns to her seat, starts writing.

Student is still shaking his leg, now starts to tap his left foot, stops writing and puts pen in his mouth. Starts to write again, shaking his right leg.

Interrupted again: Student comes in late. I explain he has to make up assignment.

Many students are starting to proofread their papers, revising, crossing out. No one talks. One student flexes his fingers. Now students start bringing their papers up to the desk. Time is up.

Still no talking.

(Student shaking his leg wrote one-half page.)

10/21/82: A Reflection on 10/14/82 Observation

This is my first observation of an 11/12 class, and the first time I've observed students writing under pressure. I didn't observe that the students were tense or nervous; they've done this type of assignment two previous times in this class. What comes to my mind is the ease, or ability to adapt to a comfortable position for writing. For me, it's important to have a certain type of "space" in order to be comfortable—to feel somewhat alone or distanced from the crowd. In fact, during my observations I sit at a relatively uncluttered and often empty table.

The students, however, seem very comfortable in creating/adapting to their own "space." Somewhere I read that students in formal/school-incorporated writing classes aren't given an opportunity to experience writing in solitude. The writer suggested that the students' inability to experience writing in a quiet, solitary environment caused them to compose poorly, and also to develop poor attitudes about writing. This is an interesting point for me:

1. About half of my students said they *enjoyed/required* quiet when asked to describe how they write.

2. Whenever I've told students to spread out, make themselves comfortable, and write, they have selected various niches in the room—in corners, under tables, behind chairs and dividers, etc.

3. This particular class seemed to establish barriers by positioning themselves in certain ways—arms on tables, heads resting on curved arms, bodies hunched over their papers.

4. The students sitting at the table with the boy who alternates between shaking his left and right leg while writing with his

left hand don't appear to notice his movement. Yet he was driving me crazy! I could just imagine the table vibrating.

Spelling surfaces again! I wonder if the students realized my different treatment and reaction to the two students who asked how to spell words? I'm sure the boy I told to get a dictionary noticed! I remember thinking how I wanted to be sure to record accurately his frustration and the way he approached the dictionary to look up his word. However, in the midst of this thought, I was interrupted by another problem speller. By the time I finished scribbling the word, the first student had looked up his word, and resumed writing! Now *I* was frustrated!!

(From the log of Marion MacLean, high school English teacher, 1981–82)

10/28/81

I am seeing something unsettling in myself. I can't "grade" any more. It's spooky. What I mean is that I can't put *grades* on students' papers (rough drafts, anyway). I realized that when I kept putting off grading my papers—the *Oedipus* essays that were the first biggies the AP kids have done in this year's class. I kept thinking, "Well, I have to let them know what I think of where their papers stand." But, I reasoned, they will see where they stand from my comments. The only way, though, that I could conceive of putting grades on the papers was to let the grade reflect where the paper was in its development—in the *writing process.* An F for those papers that were just beginning, for instance. But I could see that the only reason they'd be *F* papers was that they *were* just beginning—and the *A* papers (there were none because I was looking at rough drafts and not any finished papers, not even in terms of idea development) would just have been those at the end of the process.

I don't know. I wonder now if that's what I was doing: failing beginning papers, giving *C*s to papers about halfway done, putting *A*s on the ones most finished. *Is that what grades reflect?*

Log entries are the first pieces of writing that the teachers bring to share with their small support groups and to submit for comments by the leaders. We ask the teachers to give us copies (not the originals) of selected entries that they feel need the leader's response. Eventually, the logs contain the following:

1. descriptions of events and interactions that occur in the classroom

2. miscellaneous interruptions, behavior and management problems, teaching plans, fleeting thoughts, and stray details that contribute to an understanding of the context of the research

3. bits of conversation, phrases overheard from students or other people and jotted down quickly either during or after class

4. surprises, puzzling things that seem unexplainable or unexpected

5. reflections on what is happening—speculative writings full of questions and tentative hypotheses about certain events

6. reflections after rereading log entries—attempts to see connections and patterns in the research, attempts at shaping the focus of the research question, and attempts at analysis

7. thoughts and reactions to the research process itself, to what teachers are noticing in themselves, their thinking, and their reactions to the research readings and the group

Teacher-researchers write in their logs as often as they can: while students are writing, during a few minutes of break, after school, or while they are interviewing students about their writing. The logs serve as the records of the teachers' questions, observations, and reflections.

Discussion and Support Groups

The teacher-researcher group is subdivided into smaller groups of four or five that are organized on the basis of suggestions from the participating teachers. In general, subgroups cut across grade levels and disciplines. How the groups are formed is not as important as the fact that they meet regularly and allow the participants time to get to know each other and each other's work. When the groups meet, they read and discuss their research logs, data, attempts at analysis and findings, and drafts of articles.

Group members hear their own work read and discussed, see and hear what other teachers are doing, and support each other throughout the research process, both professionally and personally. The group's supportive atmosphere makes it possible for teachers to be honest about what goes on in their classes, about both the problems and the successes, which seem equally hard for them to discuss openly. The groups also validate the members' research data and analysis by questioning and offering a variety of interpretations in addition to those of the researchers. Group members do not compete with each other. There seems to be no "turf" jealousy, but instead a cooperative delight in—and sometimes corroboration of—each other's findings.

The larger group also serves a supportive role. Discussions of readings and presentations by guest researchers take place in the large group meetings. Much discussion also occurs during the mid-session refreshment break and moves across the lines of the smaller groups. At the time of the publication deadline, each teacher gives a short talk to the whole group about his or her research, tracing its progress, citing its findings, and addressing the group's questions.

When the teacher-researchers give their ten-minute oral reports, the other teachers in the group ask questions and express interest in the work, often remarking on each other's studies as they begin to see connections and pointing out common questions or different findings. Until this time, most have not yet heard the details of the research being conducted by teacher-researchers outside of their small group: they have been immersed in the work of their own groups' members. These oral reports serve as the final synthesis of the teacher-researchers' work and sometimes result in last-minute revisions of the articles.

At this time we also distribute information on entering articles in the ERIC system and on calls for manuscripts from professional journals. We encourage members of the group to publish beyond the class booklet, which is an inexpensive, photocopied collection arranged alphabetically by author.

Group Leaders

The essential work of the leaders of the teacher-researcher group is to organize the meetings and respond to the work that the teachers are doing while providing working models of teacher-researchers.

From what we know of the experience of being teacher-researchers, we believe that it is important for the leaders of such a group to be teacher-researchers in their own classrooms. Although we don't know the outcome of groups whose leaders have never been teacher-researchers, our direct experience so deeply informs our leadership of the group that it is hard to imagine being able to work confidently out of any other context. We also encourage leaders to engage in classroom research during the process of leading the group of teacher-researchers, either in that group itself or in other classes they may teach.

Group leaders respond to each person's work with interest and respect that person's ultimate authority. They speak their minds when necessary, giving their advice without pretense and allowing for other options.

Specifically, group leaders respond in their class discussions, in their individual conferences with teacher-researchers after class or on the telephone, and in their written comments on log entries, selected data, and drafts of articles. During the first year of the course, it happened that the interval between class meetings resulted in teachers receiving comments about their work two weeks after they had turned in the log entries. While this was a matter of concern to the group leader at first, the delay actually led to an increase in the teacher-researchers' confidence. Having turned in their work for comment, having discussed the work with the support group, and needing to proceed, the group members made their own decisions. The leader's comments often became affirmations of the teachers' decisions about their research.

Example 3: Responses from Group Leaders

(From Marian Mohr, group leader and high school English teacher, to Meg Gibson, high school Latin and English teacher, 1981–82)
Oct. 14—I'm intrigued by the "note passing." How do you think it's working out? You've gotten some efficient new ways to handle it, I think, such as having both your letter and the student's on one sheet.

Your final statement is interesting. Do you have any idea *why* the students want you to pick the letter topics?

Nov. 23—I really appreciated the lengthy entry from 11/11 and I think you're right about the publishing. What interested me especially was what you noticed about the ESL student. With academically unsuccessful students I sometimes want to hurry them along too fast, forgetting how many years of failure are weighing in on us both. I like your idea of focusing on the data. Could you develop a list of *broad* topics to use in this kind of writing, ones that can be handled in several ways? Or, always give them a choice of topics? There are a lot of ways to handle the topic problem and still build in choice. I'm eager to read the letters. How many will you study in depth? Interviews?

Dec. 13—I love the revision of your letter. I enjoyed the time spent talking with you and Betty on Dec. 2. Don't have much to add.

Jan. 4—You don't really have to prove anything about the letters; just analyze them and show what's there. I know what you mean about having time to *look* at the data. Did you ask the students (I think you did) to write about how they felt about the letter writing?

Example 4: Responses to Group Leaders

(Response from Ann Sevcik, high school psychology teacher, to a question from Marion MacLean, group leader and high school English teacher, 1984–85)

Last Thursday when you said, "What are you going to do next?" I really wasn't ready, partly because I was about 80 percent of the way through the first round of data and partly because, like a dope, I hadn't given it the *first* thought. "What *next?*" indeed! "What's happening *NOW?*" was the question last week. "What does it mean?" developed as I began to sense a shape in my data, and finally, "What am I going to do next?" surfaced as a meaningful endeavor (?) only this morning (Sunday). In the future, instead of taking up group time as I did Thursday, I wonder if I'll be able to say, "I'm not ready for that question yet. I'm still back on 'What do I have?' and 'What does it mean?'." I really enjoyed getting the feedback on "What do I have?" when I read those student insights, and I found the discussion about owning learning to be crucial in helping me formulate a "What does it mean?" conjecture. I wish I had been ready then to answer what I'd do next, but I surely wasn't. I'll try to get in step—synchronized?

(Reaction of Anne Wotring, high school English teacher, to a response from Marian Mohr, 1981–82)

Re: your comment about "almost *all* elementary kids doing think-writing when they begin to write." I'm not so sure about that. I think that the books they learn to read from are *not* thoughtful and therefore, may give them the idea that the writing they do is not supposed to be thoughtful either. Also, they get hung up on thinking about spelling and grammar, which impedes thinking about content. I think with Don Graves as a teacher, they may be think-writing, but I wonder about what most students do. I think Graves shows us the fluency that small children *can* attain, but do most attain it when they may have misinformation about what writing is?

I believe this because I think that's what happened to me. . . .

I am fascinated by the think-talking that Piaget and Vygotsky called egocentric speech and its importance in development. I see that children need to be encouraged to do think-writing in elementary school for its importance in their development as writers, thinkers, and learners.

Maybe I'm wrong but I think the lettering, handwriting, spelling, and reading lessons stop *most* elementary kids from doing think-writing, which probably could come as naturally as egocentric speech does in babies.

So, I agree that *all* elementary kids could do think-writing, but I don't think that they are doing it. I think this writing has helped me clarify what I want to know.

(Response from Betsy Sanford, elementary school teacher, to comments in a class meeting, 1984–85)

Boy, do I have a lot cooking tonight! There are two, possibly three, issues I haven't even addressed yet. I'll mention them, but won't expand on all of them, I'm sure:

1. Marian's comment in class tonight that bothered me.

2. Why I'm not typing this entry.

3. What Joan said in my group tonight about every choice being a revision, and what she said about how you'd never ask a kid to write and then revise immediately, and my reactions to that.

4. How it seems clear that I don't want to do a case study on Tracey; how I should have known that from my recent behavior; and how comfortable I feel about Marques and Jenna being my case studies.

5. Why I note the time the way I do in my log. *First of all*: Marion's (no, *Marian's*) comment during our discussion of the articles. She noted, during the end of the discussion, that we were seemingly quite focused on the *content* of the articles we're reading, rather than the *way* the research was done or the way it was reported.

On the way home tonight (and even *as* Marian commented on it, quite naturally), I felt as if I had missed the boat about something, that I had been not being a good student, or (the dreaded problem—I had not been *smart* enough to be a good student), that I should have had a different perspective about the articles. I see the point (even this soon) so clearly, that Marian saw us as not looking as *researchers* at research articles. But only in the very most vague way could I have dealt with those articles as a researcher looking at the research write-up of other researchers before now.

I have a theory. (This is for you two, Marian and Marion, as well as me): We are just at the point that we are facing big issues in our work, since we are just now needing to come to grips with *what* our questions are, and we are praying that we have already collected and can collect enough data by December 13 to get things off the ground. You were asking us, at the same time as we were feeling rather out-of-step or out-of-kilter, to perceive ourselves as bona fide, legitimate researchers who would interact with the structure and form of these researchers' papers.

You know what *my* reaction to those papers was?

It was: Gimme content! (As in: "If I ever needed content, I *need it now!* Tell me what to look for in my *own* work.") And so, this *might* be what was going on tonight, Marian. It is what was going on for me. I thought you might want to know.

Addenda:

6. Ideas I had about my next step or steps.

7. There *was* a 7, but I can't remember it (it came and went *so* quickly!). And now Kennie's home, and I'm going to watch the Redskins game with him. Maybe I'll address #2–6 or #2–7 tomorrow. And maybe not . . . we'll see.

As teacher-researchers, the group leaders must also question their own assumptions and suspend personal judgments, thereby demonstrating such a stance for the group members. They must continually inquire about the broad range of educational research. As leaders, we found it necessary to expand our knowledge of educational research beyond what we knew of quantitative theory and methodology. The following books have shaped our understanding of qualitative and ethnographic theory and methods in educational research:

Agar, M. 1980. *The professional stranger.* New York: Academic Press.

Cooper, C.R., and L. Odell, eds. 1978. *Research on composing: Points of departure.* Urbana, Ill.: National Council of Teachers of English.

Erickson, F. 1979. On standards of descriptive validity in studies of classroom activity. Occasional paper no. 16. East Lansing, Mich.: Institute for Research on Teaching.

Glaser, B., and A. Strauss. 1967. *The discovery of grounded theory: Strategies of qualitative research.* Chicago: Aldine.

Goetz, J., and M. LeCompte. 1984. *Ethnography and qualitative design in educational research.* New York: Academic.

Guba, E.G. 1978. *Toward a methodology of naturalistic inquiry in educational evaluation.* Los Angeles: Center for the Study of Evaluation, University of California.

Lofland, J., and L. Lofland. 1984. *Analyzing social settings: A guide to qualitative observation and analysis.* 2d ed. Belmont, Calif.: Davis Wadsworth.

Nixon, J. 1981. *A teacher's guide to action research.* London: Grant McIntyre.

Rudduck, J., and D. Hopkins, eds. 1985. *Research as a basis for teaching: Readings from the work of Lawrence Stenhouse.* Portsmouth, N.H.: Heinemann.

In addition to their own reading, leaders should provide articles for group discussion and organize a forum for the discussion of issues concerning teacher-researchers within the research community. (Some suggested articles on these topics are listed in the following section entitled "Readings.")

We want to encourage those who lead a group of teacher-researchers to develop a bibliography and look to their own mentors. Certain researchers, especially Donald Graves, Dixie Goswami, Evelyn Jacobs, Pat D'Arcy, and Ken Kantor, have been examples to us in their approaches to research as well as in their encouragement of teacher-researchers. Marie Wilson Nelson has also provided regular and welcome support as a guest researcher during our discussion of data analysis.

The list of people and readings included here is highly selective and reflects our personal needs as group leaders. Much of the history of teacher-researchers is yet to be written, and the habit of inquiry that characterizes successful teacher-researcher leaders should help them to discover mentors and bibliographic material appropriate for them and their groups.

Readings

Teacher-researchers are not necessarily trying to amass a knowledge of all the research completed in their area of interest. They do not usually begin with a literature search; they start by looking at what is most interesting to them. The subject may be one that other group members have found interesting too, but because each teacher-researcher and his or her classroom is unique, each person will have a different perspective on what he or she chooses to study.

The reading that goes on during the research process is about research, language, learning, and teaching. Teachers also read on their own to add to their knowledge of the subject they are studying. The bibliography for students of writing compiled by Sam Watson, director of the University of North Carolina at Charlotte Writing Project, is distributed to members of the group early in the research process. Other bibliographies are made available, and teachers frequently exchange articles with each other or share articles they think the group should read. These readings help the teacher-researchers individually and provide a sense of the history and the closeness of the research community.

The list of readings we include here is limited and selective rather than comprehensive. It represents the kinds of works we choose for the whole group to read and discuss together. We classify the articles in six categories and try to time the reading to coincide with the teacher-researchers' needs during the research process. (See Appendix A for a sample list of readings for one year's group.)

Although we want other teacher-researchers to see some of the articles that have been helpful to us, we think it is important for each group to devise its own lists from the constantly growing body of work by and about teacher-researchers. Our suggestions, classified and in sequence, follow.

We begin with articles that help teachers get used to the idea of qualitative research being different from experimental or quantitative research. We begin here because most teachers have had little or no experience with qualitative research and because we think that qualitative research methodology is well suited to the teacher-researcher's situation. Some articles that may be helpful in the beginning are the following:

Eisner, E. 1984. Can educational research inform educational practice? *Phi Delta Kappan* 65:447–52.

Graves, D. 1980. A new look at writing research. *Language Arts* 57:913–19.

Graves, D. 1981. Writing research for the eighties: What is needed. *Language Arts* 58:197–206.

Graves, D. 1981. Where have all the teachers gone? *Language Arts* 58:492–97. The three Graves articles are published as one essay under the title "A New Look at Research on Writing" in *Perspectives on Writing in Grades 1–8* (Urbana, Ill.: National Council of Teachers of English, 1981) and in *A Researcher Learns to Write* (Exeter, N.H.: Heinemann, 1984).

We also include articles, such as Judith Langer's "Musings" from the May 1984 issue of *Research in the Teaching of English* (vol. 18, 117–18), which address issues in educational research that we think are important for classroom teachers to acknowledge in the broader context of research in the teaching of English.

The next group of readings addresses the role of the teacher as a researcher and develops an understanding of research as a process.

Atwell, N. 1982. Class-based writing research: Teachers learn from students. *English Journal* 71:84–87.

Goswami, D., and P.R. Stillman, eds. 1987. *Reclaiming the classroom: Teacher research as an agency for change.* Upper Montclair, N.J.: Boynton/Cook.

Hoagland, N. 1984. On becoming a teacher-researcher: An introduction to qualitative research. *The Writing Instructor:* 55–59.

Mohr, M. 1980. The teacher as researcher. *Virginia English Bulletin* 30 (2): 61–64.

To address the process of research, we use articles concerning the emergent nature of research, articles commenting on the research processes of prominent researchers, and articles addressing different activities that occur during the various periods of the research. Of the readings that follow, the MacLean and the Wotring and Tierney selections show teacher-researchers' processes while the Loflands and Perl discuss research processes in a more general context.

Lofland, J., and L. Lofland. 1984. 2d ed. Analyzing data. Chapter 9 in *Analyzing social settings: A guide to qualitative observation and analysis.* Belmont, Calif.: Davis Wadsworth.

MacLean, M. 1983. Voices within: The audience speaks. *English Journal* 72 (7): 62–66.

Perl, S. 1979. Research as discovery. Speech given as Promising Researcher at the National Council of Teachers of English Annual Convention, San Francisco, Calif.

Wotring, A.M., and R. Tierney. 1981. *Two studies of writing in high school science.* Berkeley, Calif.: Bay Area Writing Project.

The next category of readings includes those that raise questions about assumptions underlying particular theories as well as those that underlie different kinds of classroom research. Among the theoretical articles that we have used are the following:

Emig, J. 1983. Non-magical thinking. In *The web of meaning.* Upper Montclair, N.J.: Boynton/Cook.

Heath, S. B. 1980. The functions and uses of literacy. *Journal of Communications* 30 (1): 123–33.

Moffett, J. 1983. Reading and writing as meditation. *Language Arts* 60: 315–23.

We examine the assumptions behind the collection of particular kinds of data and the reports that may follow. We include articles that show differing degrees of analysis. Comparing a very selective case study with a broad survey may help to reveal which aspect of each can be useful.

Kamler, B. 1980. One child, one teacher, one classroom: The story of one piece of writing. *Language Arts* 57:680–93.

Moran, C. 1981. Reading literature/writing literature. *College Composition and Communication* 32:21–29.

Newkirk, T., and N. Atwell, eds. 1982. *Understanding writing: Ways of observing, learning, and teaching.* Chelmsford, Mass.: NEREX.

Stallard, C. K. 1974. An analysis of the writing behavior of good student writers. *Research in the Teaching of English* 8:206–18.

Stallard, C. K. 1982. The composing processes of upper-level college students. In *Writing processes of college students.* Fairfax, Va.: George Mason University.

Especially during the second part of the year, we read reports that other teacher-researchers have written. While some of the discussion centers on the implications of the research in the reports, the teachers begin to notice how other researchers have selected their final areas of focus, what kinds of data may have been set aside, how context becomes a part of the final report, and how the reports present data, methodology, findings, and implications.

We try to introduce these articles late enough so that the group feels informed by them but not undermined. The articles do not serve as direct models for a teacher's report; instead, we look at their features and characteristics analytically. We select articles by teachers working on a variety of grade levels and in a variety of disciplines.

Estabrook, I. W. 1982. Talking about writing—developing independent writers. *Language Arts* 59:696–706.

Giacobbe, M. E. 1981. Kids can write the first week of school. *Learning* 10 (2): 132–33.

Grumbacher, J. 1987. Writing to learn in physics. In *The journal book,* ed. T. Fulwiler. Montclair, N.J.: Boynton/Cook.

Hauser, C. 1986. The writer's inside story. *Language Arts* 63:153–59.

McKay, L. 1986. Gaining control through commentary. *English Journal* 75: 58–62.

Womble, G. 1984. Process and processor. *English Journal* 73 (1): 34–37. A version of this article appears in *Writing-on-line: Using computers in the teaching of writing,* ed. James L. Collins and Elizabeth A. Sommers. Montclair, N.J.: Boynton/Cook, 1985.

In addition to articles that may serve as comparative examples for their research reports, teachers also refer to the following articles as they work on their drafts. These articles discuss writing about research.

Graves, D. 1984. Sixty minutes 1 and 2. In *A researcher learns to write: Selected articles and monographs.* Exeter, N.H.: Heinemann.

Macrorie, K. 1980. *Searching writing.* Montclair, N.J.: Boynton/Cook.

Murray, D. M. 1982. Write research to be read. In *Learning by teaching: Selected articles on writing and teaching.* Montclair, N.J.: Boynton/Cook.

The list of books in the section on group leaders is a helpful bibliography for all teacher-researchers, especially those who want more information on research methodology in general or on writing research methodology in particular.

Practice and Process

"Patty said, 'So we're your guinea pigs.' I responded, 'I hope not, because guinea pigs don't really react with the researcher. And I need your responses and your awareness in this!' "

Choice and the Emergent Research Question

It is essential that teachers choose freely the areas of their investigation. They come to research with areas of concern or curiosity—questions about their teaching and their students' learning. Although the initial focus may remain the same, teachers spend hours carefully refining their chosen question. They determine its boundaries, study its complexity, and analyze their relationship to it.

At first, teacher-researchers may worry about whether someone has "already done" the research they hope to pursue. Usually, as they begin to acknowledge the authority inherent in their own observations, questions, and reflections, they see that it is precisely this rich, context-specific description and analysis by teachers and students that classroom research has to offer to the research community.

Halfway through the process, the teacher-researchers read through their data and then set it aside for a period of about two weeks, the duration of winter break. After this separation, they restate the questions they are asking, which helps them review what they have done and project into the analytical work ahead. Even though they start with a basic question or area of concern (often phrased, "What happens when. . . ?" or "How does . . . work?"), many feel that it is not until the writing of the final report that they "know" what it is that they have been trying to discover.

Example 5: Teachers Shaping Research Questions

(Log entries from Mary Schulman, elementary school teacher, 1981–82)

23

12/7/81

I do still feel as if I'm groping in the dark. I hope that's not abnormal for a researcher, especially at this stage of the game. I keep thinking I should know where I'm going, but I don't. I'm thinking I should have more data. I have my journal writings and writing samples and I'm going to go with the questions and maybe some taping of conferences.

Why conferences?

Let's see—something important—I'm interested in the conference. It's a valuable tool in helping children learn to write and to improve their writing.

But what facet would be worthwhile exploring?

Good question.

1/17/82

I was driving home from school today and seemingly out of nowhere a question did occur. I wondered what would happen if a group of my second graders had conferences with a group of my first graders about their writing(s)? What kinds of questions will my second graders ask? Will my first graders revise their writings? Will their writing improve? How? Will the conferences the second graders have with the first graders influence or affect how they confer with their own group? Will their conference techniques improve? Will their writing improve? What revisions will they make on their own writing(s)?

(Excerpt from Mary Schulman's article, 1982)

When I began this study, I knew that I was interested in learning more about how beginning writers write and the actual use of conferences with beginning writers in the process of writing. This includes the types of questions I asked during the prewriting, composing, and rewriting stages of the writing process. My question became: "What types of conference responses or questions does a teacher make or ask beginning writers?"

There can be nothing about this work—including the first decision of whether to join the group at all—that is not chosen. Throughout the process, it is the teacher who chooses the course to follow, the direction that the inquiry will take. Directed by classroom necessities, by speculations, and sometimes by intuitive and apparently unplanned activities that become turning points in the research, the process of any one teacher's research originates from the teacher and that teacher's context.

Since researchers under these circumstances inevitably end up examining themselves, they have to be in control of their search in order to accept their own observation. They have to feel safe enough to look closely at themselves. This safety, in large part, comes from the nonjudgmental and analytical stance that is crucial to this work and from having that stance affirmed both by their small groups and by the group's leaders.

Observation and Reflection

Observation and reflection are the foundation of the teacher-researcher's work in the classroom. The very first entries in the research log are observations of a class at work. Although the observations may not seem to reveal much to most teachers as they begin them (a log entry frequently includes the questions, "Why am I doing this?" and "Am I doing this right?"), they are fruitful activities in many ways. Teachers who observe and write about their students' writing begin to speculate on those students who raise their heads and stare into space, those who stop writing, reread, and then continue, or those who are constantly crossing out and replacing words. Each of these observations can lead to a question for research. Because thinking and learning (and, of course, writing) involve so much that is unseen, observing the outward evidence is a logical place to begin.

It is difficult for some teachers to be observers because they are accustomed to giving suggestions or deciding on the spot what is going on and responding accordingly. As they observe, the reasons for student behavior seem more complicated. Suddenly, teachers see situations as having more variables than they had acknowledged previously.

Observing is especially helpful to teachers who have students and classes that present management and behavior problems. When observed and reflected upon as data, a student's behavior takes on a meaning different than it has when judged as a result of a teacher's preconceived ideas about its causes and outcomes. Teacher-researchers do not, of course, allow their classrooms to fall apart as they write in their logs. They may, however, report a change in their management styles away from quick reactions and toward more questioning and listening.

Example 6: Ways in Which Observation and Reflection Affect Management and Teaching Strategies

(From Alberta Grossman's log, 1981–82)

Many of the problems the students are experiencing finding information and getting started I attribute to me. I feel as if I ought to have been organizing and prearranging more for them. On the other hand it's not easy in our school with our librarians; there is not a sense of being welcomed.

But maybe organizing is actually contraindicated. After all, the thesis of I-Search is that the interest in the quest facilitates the quest. (But let us not kid ourselves; the research itself is often an anxiety-producing drag. Witness some of my own feelings while doing research on evaluating writing—even though there was basic curiosity and much satisfaction.)

What if the teacher's own need for closure forces kids to take the path of least resistance?

Reflections become the first attempts at analysis, and the teacher-researcher logs, as ongoing documents of classroom life, slowly start to point toward the findings that eventually result. It is not unusual for a teacher-researcher to discover an early log entry with the hunch or clue that later becomes a fully developed finding.

Example 7: A Reflection Leading toward Analysis

(From the log of Courtney Rogers, high school English teacher, 1983–84)
9/29/83: Reflection on 9/21 Observation

I have probably waited too long to do this reflection but rereading it takes me back fairly well.

I wonder about the physical act (acts? action?) of writing. Some of the individuals look totally engaged and absorbed at times, but I wonder how it differs for each. I think about occasions when I have been mentally engaged in the writing, mainly so that the physical act of getting the words down seems really secondary, and even a hindrance—I can't write fast enough. On other occasions I recall focusing more on the physical act of writing: watching my pen move across the page, the thoughts temporarily at least taking a back seat to the forming of letters and words on the page. I wonder what the relationship of these two is—for myself—for them. (Is this what I'm supposed to be doing in this reflection or am I getting too far off base?)

Gina and Lynn I described very similarly in the physical act of writing, yet knowing what I do about their apparent abilities, I wonder if the same thing is going on for both of them. Both appear extremely engrossed in what they are doing, yet I find myself wondering if Lynn is more mentally engaged and Gina more physically engaged in the act of writing. Thinking about that, my question seems ill-placed. My suspicion is that both happen for all writers, I guess.

How did Elizabeth get started, considering she didn't feel creative—I interpret that as not in the mood to be mentally engaged. Could the physical act of writing stimulate the mental activity? I think—or know (I think!) that that has happened to me.

Data Collection

Data collection consists of much more than log entries and classroom descriptions. In an effort to compile a wide range of data, teacher-researchers distribute student questionnaires, analyze students' papers and comments, and conduct in-depth interviews with students.

Questionnaires and Surveys

Teachers frequently start out with a survey or questionnaire that gives a broad base for understanding, a profile that may result in a more specific study. These surveys are sometimes spontaneous, emerging out of a class discussion. Or, they may consist of one or two questions a teacher decides to ask students to respond to in writing.

The surveys are compiled in a variety of ways, sometimes by counting certain answers, sometimes by looking for recurring ideas or statements, and sometimes holistically, as a basis for further questions of the class or individual students. The advantage teacher-researchers have in the use of survey data is that they return to the takers of the survey every day and can find out what the students mean by their answers.

Example 8: Surveys and Questionnaires

(Veronica Brown's draft of a survey, 1982–83)

(Possible) Survey of Students' Attitudes toward Writing

Is this a valid way to collect data about students' experiences/ attitudes about writing?

Always Sometimes Never

1. Do you like to write?
2. Do you write at home outside of class?
3. Do you worry about spelling when you write?
4. Do members of your family write?
5. Have your written a lot in school?
6. Have your teachers generally praised you for your writing?
7. Do you like to share your writings with others?
8. Are you a good writer?
9. Do you believe there is a purpose for writing?
10. Do you have a favorite writer?
11. Do you read as much as you write?
12. Has your writing improved over the years?
13. Has your writing improved in the last month?
14. Do you write best in quiet or noisy situations?
15. Do your English grades accurately reflect your writing ability?
16. Do you hate to write?
17. Does your teacher grade you on mechanical or grammatical errors?
18. Are you graded on your ideas?
19. Do you like to comment on others' writing?

(Questionnaire by Dottie Feldman, high school English teacher, 1984–85)

Name _____ Period _____
English 12—Mrs. Feldman

Evaluation Questionnaire

1. Do you think most teachers are "fair graders"? Why or why not?
2. Do you think that you can become a "fair grader"?
3. How should a teacher grade/evaluate a paper?
4. When a teacher grades/evaluates a paper, what kind of feedback to the student is helpful?
5. Do you like grading your own papers, or does it make you uncomfortable?
6. What help would you like in being an objective evaluator?
7. What follow-up would you like after a peer has evaluated your work? After a teacher has evaluated it? After you have evaluated it?

Example 9: Questionnaire and Teacher Observation

(Questionnaire by Peg Culley, high school English teacher, 1984–85)
Grammar History: 9/27/84

1. Write about your history as a student of grammar. Think back to your grade school years and beyond and describe your training in grammar to date. How did you learn grammar? What are your memories about learning grammar?
2. Describe in writing what you first think or feel when you hear the statement, "Now, we will begin our study of grammar."
3. Answer one of the following:
   a. If you wrote all positive responses to question 2, can you think of and record the negative responses to grammar that you may have?
   b. If your response to question 2 was negative, can you think of and record your positive responses to the study of grammar?
4. What do you enjoy most about learning grammar?
5. What do you enjoy least about learning grammar?
6. How do you see that the study of grammar has helped you develop as a writer?

(Observation from Peg Culley's log)
9/24/84: after 1:20

I just did it. I handed out the questionnaire. All here but Cheryl (19 in). Lights are out. One unit exploded and sparked and smelled as I sat eating my lunch. I expect a maintenance man any minute. Students going up and down hall—noisy. I'll close door/open windows. . . .

I told students that I wanted their help with grammar. I explained that I will be trying something new regarding the teaching of grammar that I hope will help them learn and remember more. And since I was trying out something new, I wanted to study what they did as I tried my new teaching methods. So I was going to be a little like a scientist.

I told them first I wanted to know something about their relationship to grammar and so I was giving them a questionnaire relating to how they learned grammar.

(Chris is looking over at Matt B.'s writing.)

I asked if they had any questions. Yvonne asked—"So we will tell you about how we learned grammar?"

Patty said, "So, we're your guinea pigs." I responded, "I hope not because guinea pigs don't really interact with the researcher. And I need your responses and your awareness in this."

Student Papers

Student papers and drafts may be collected over the period of a semester or longer. Teachers collect papers as a matter of course; they do not ordinarily look at them as data to be analyzed, although they may in an informal manner as they evaluate the papers and plan their lessons. As teacher-researchers, they look at a few papers repeatedly and with great care. And, as with their observations of behavior, their close study of students' papers makes the writing process appear more complex and varied.

Student Comments

Frequently teacher-researchers ask students to reflect on what they think may be happening in their work, to write (admittedly with hindsight) about how they did something, or to try to keep track of a process as they go through it. These data are checked against and compared with other sources of information.

Teacher-researchers are conscious of the fact that students may try to please them by saying what they think the teacher wants to hear or that students may wish to do the opposite—express their anger against the classroom situation and the teacher. The advantages teacher-researchers have are their time with the students, their writings about the situation, and their research group's comments.

With this constant scrutiny, it is difficult for a teacher to conclude that "they like it" or "they don't like it." Teacher-researchers move beyond this shallow evaluation to "Why did they write this . . . think this . . . do things this way?"

Example 10: Students' Comments on Writing

(From Veronica Brown's data, 1982–83)

When I write I think an awful lot because to me, thinking is the best form of writing. How do I think thinking is a form of writing? Well if it wasn't for thinking, there would be few things written. But I also like to imagine. You know, to really go all the way, to make things more dramatic, or even to make a fairy tale so real that you start believing it.

I'm not sure if I see any changes in the way I write. To be honest I didn't know I had the ability to write the things I do. In other words, I didn't realize that I had such a talent. Well I'm not sure how to write down what I'm thinking at this point. I suppose that I have made a tremendous change in writing, or maybe I just never noticed. My eighth-grade English teacher didn't indicate whether or not a paper was well written. He just told us our mistakes and gave us our grade.

I'm not sure that it is my writing that has changed. I believe that it is my attitude toward writing, and my mind itself. My writing itself has always been there but this class brought it out. I think that has a lot to do with the journals. The topics that I was given made it quite simple to write. My attitude toward writing has changed tremendously. I now really enjoy writing; especially when someone tells me that it is good, or I receive a plus for my grade. My mind sometimes seems to be a different part of my body, but when I'm writing it knows where it should be. Now when I want to write, most of the time, I don't have to worry about getting a bad grade. I think that's how I have changed—I don't worry about the grade, I just write.

(From Marion MacLean's data, 1981–82: students' responses when asked to describe the audiences they envisioned for drafts of their college application essays)

The impression of the audience I have is a group of super-intellectuals who are perfect in every way. They would look at my scores and essay and just dump it into a huge wastebasket. They would scorn my application and countless other hopefuls. I feel that they feel they are far superior to people like me, who do not possess genius intellect, like them.

I was my audience—I really wrote for me and my close friends. I would not have sent this to a college because they would think I was illiterate. I feel like I have to get out a thesaurus if a paper is to be acceptable to the admissions people at (this university). I really don't know how to be myself and sound impressive at the same time. How do I? For some reason the stuff that I'm writing now seems like it is just play—certainly not college material. I guess I want some earth-shaking topic. I want to go to (that school), how the _____[sic] am I gonna do that with this?

In-depth Interviews

Student interviews can be an excellent data source for the teacher-researcher. We think it is important for teachers to let students know that they're interested in tape-recording their comments, letting them know why and always respecting any reservations a student might have about being recorded.

Example 11: Interviews and Reflections

(From Patty Sue Williams's work with one of her first-grade students, 1982–83)

Tape Transcript: Kim, 11/3/82

Teacher: How do you feel about writing?

Kim: I like it.

Teacher: Why do you like to write?

Kim: I guess I like to draw the pictures and write about it.

Teacher: You like to draw the pictures and write about it. Do you know what you were thinking about when you did your critter drafts? Can you tell me?

Kim: Not really.

Teacher: Do you know what you think about when you write?

Kim: I think critters.

Teacher: You were thinking about critters. What about some of these other things you wrote?

Kim: Well . . . . I don't know.

Teacher: Here's yesterday's. What were you thinking about when you did that one?

Kim: A unicorn in the woods.

Teacher: A unicorn in the woods. What do you know about unicorns?

Kim: Well, they're just like horses, but they have a horn.

Teacher: O.K. Do you remember when you first heard about a unicorn?

Kim: I forgot . . . long time ago.

Teacher: Do you remember why you got interested in horses?

Kim: They're so pretty! I like them 'cause they're furry. I have a horse at this farm. Her name's Sheila and she's like a little Shetland pony. She'll stay like a little pony because she's a Shetland pony. Shetland ponies stay like a little pony.

Teacher: Where is this horse?

Kim: Up at _____'s farm. She lives in Manassas. I love going up there.

Teacher: How often do you go up there?

Kim: Well, not very much. It gets very dusty up there, lots of ragweed and hay that I'm allergic to. I'm not allergic to horses, but when they breathe out of their nose like this (demonstrates), that's what I'm allergic to. They're so pretty.

Teacher: Do you like to write about anything else?

Kim: Sometimes I like to write about cats or dogs but I like unicorns, horses, and Pegasus more.

Teacher: Pegasus? That's a myth, right? A story about a horse a long time ago. *That* Pegasus?

Kim: Yes, the flying horse, *that* Pegasus!

Teacher: How'd you hear about him?

Kim: Well . . . I have this Wonder Book about horses, and I saw one on TV, but I had the book before. One page has a picture of Pegasus. My mommy told me one time when I was leaving the farm . . . I saw the show Pegasus. My aunt works in J.C. Penney's in the toy department. They have this little toy Pegasus. His wings come off, so he can be a regular horse, or Pegasus. I might get it for my report card, if it's good. (K. sighed like a horse.)

Teacher: You *sound* like a horse!

Kim: I got good horse sounds, too. I guess I like when they rear. In the first page of my Wonder Book, when you first open it up, there's this rearing horse and I trace him.

Teacher: Is that how you learned to draw or paint a rearing horse, because you've been tracing one?

Kim: Yeah! I got one book about a horse: *Knots in the Rope.* I got this zoo book. It's got zebras in it. I like zebras, too. They look like horses except they have stripes.

Teacher: You're really into horses, aren't you? Do you go riding? Do you have special clothes for riding?

Kim: No. But every time you ride, you've got to have pants on. But I never get to ride Sheila. You know why? 'Cause you got to learn to saddle a horse by yourself.

Teacher: That's the rule, huh?

Kim: I can carry a saddle, but I can't lift it up, buckle it and stuff. I put reins on pretty well.

Teacher: You put the reins on?

Kim: They're really called a bridle . . . I got the Barbie doll horse "Dallas." I wash Dallas's mane and tail . . . Can I bring my horses tomorrow?

Teacher: Sure! We'd like to see what you write about all the time.

Kim: Well, true. You know that other horse I brought? It's a stallion. . . .

Reaction to transcript and conferences, 11/4/82

I feel this transcript is an important key into Kim's metacognition as well as how prose models have influenced her writing. I need to "cogitate" on why.

The other children are most anxious to be "interviewed" about their writing folders.

(I have discovered a new way to preserve an original draft but clean it up enough for a parent to type it into a book. The students use a colored marker and make the changes as we confer. No rewriting except to put on the chart. They choose the colored marker from a special set they also use to illustrate published books.)

I am so gratified at how the skills are being taught and reinforced via the writing conference. For example: today in our conference I saw that April had spelled *they* "thay." When I told her the correct spelling she reminded me "ay" spells the sound "a." She is the same child who spelled *busy* "bizy" and was astounded when I told her, "You won't believe this, but busy is spelled b-u-s-y."

I'm too tired to write any more.

(From Mary Schulman's work with a first-grade student, 1981–82)
Kimberly's story: November 12

(Interview)

Kimberly: Look . . . want me read it?

Teacher: Oh, yes!

[Text: I wK t A s]

Kimberly: I want togoon a swing

  (Kimberly points, trying to make the talk and graphics match.)

Teacher: Oh . . . .

Kimberly: That's me [points to figure on right]. Those are the swings at King's Dominion [an amusement park]. My mom took us there.

Teacher: You got to ride the swings at King's Dominion? Who went with you and your mom?

Kimberly: My sister.

Teacher: I bet you had fun.

Kimberly: We went on lots of rides . . . but I like the swings the most.

Teacher: Why?

Kimberly: 'Cause they go high and fast.

Teacher: Wow... they go high and fast. Will you add that?

Kimberly: No, I don't want to.

Teacher: Tell me ... why did you cross out here ... and here? [I pointed to the first two lines.]

Kimberly: 'Cause you do that when you write.

Teacher: Oh ... I see. This is a good try writing "I want to go on a swing." I want to show you something.

Lightly in pencil, I wrote "I want to go on a swing." under Kimberly's writing. I said, "Look how close you are." I pointed to Kimberly's written text and then to my text, and began: "Look, you have the word 'I'... you left a space after the word 'I'... you have the 'w' in the word 'want'... the 't' in 'to'... and the 's' in 'swing.' You know, you have most of the beginning letters in the words you wrote!"

Kimberly smiled.

Additional Sources

Other sources of data might be writing folders kept by students, records of student group meetings about their writing, and discussions by the whole class. Although they may study a few cases in depth, teacher-researchers are always looking at data from all their students in the course of their daily work. This view of the whole picture helps them to ground their opinions continually. They analyze as they work, moving repeatedly from the whole to the focus on their individual students or group of students.

Because their research and their teaching are so closely connected, teacher-researchers do not "conduct research" as if it were something unusual or additional to their normal work. The data students provide are the writing and discussing they do as part of their classwork.

The students themselves are data of a different kind. They notice that their learning processes are important not only to describe and recognize but also to change and diversify. During the writing of the final report, students often act as an additional revision group for the teacher-researcher. They listen to the teachers' drafts and validate or question findings, and they may return to their teachers with additional ideas about their writing or learning, because they have recognized that how they learn is important. They become co-researchers with the teacher-researcher, a relationship that both simplifies and intensifies the problem of confidentiality in the research.

Teacher-researchers are eager to give the students recognition for their contributions to the research, and students are generally pleased to be part of a possible publication. They may choose their own "research" names for the reports since in some cases teacher-researchers choose not to use students' real names. And, if teacher-researchers are using students' works or comments in an article for publication, students should be asked for their written consent that the materials be used. Parental consent should be obtained if the students are under eighteen years old.

Example 12: Students as Collaborating Researchers

(From Alberta Grossman's log, 1981–82)

I read my students my report of what we had just done. Good response. The first thing they said before I began was, "You're not going to use our names, are you?" They were pleased that I had changed their names. Mickey made a little fuss. "That means I have big ears" but then he decided he liked it. He also responded to "People don't learn from absorbing. They learn from mucking around and finding out for themselves." He said, "See, you finally learned it."

Most teacher-researchers have four or five sources of data to compare and contrast as they look for valid interpretations. They also have the advantages of conducting ongoing analysis and reflecting continually in their logs about their data. Finally, they have the helpful and watchful eyes of their research groups and group leaders to question their interpretations and to suggest different ones.

Analysis and Interpretation

It is difficult to believe that a collection of data will eventually make some kind of sense; accepting the apparent lack of controls at the start and trusting that patterns will emerge are big hurdles. Although roughly the first half of the year is planned as data collection and the second half as analysis of data and writing the report, analysis is also part of the ongoing effort to make sense of the observations and data as they are being collected. Even though teachers have been regularly writing reflections that lead to analysis, speculation, and theory formation, the analytical work that begins about halfway through the year's process involves a new effort to see their work as a whole. In order to help teacher-researchers see emergent patterns and connections, we ask them to do two things: to draw a picture, chart, or diagram of their data as a whole and to write what they think their findings are at the halfway mark.

Example 13: Visualizing Analysis

(From Courtney Rogers's data, 1983–84)

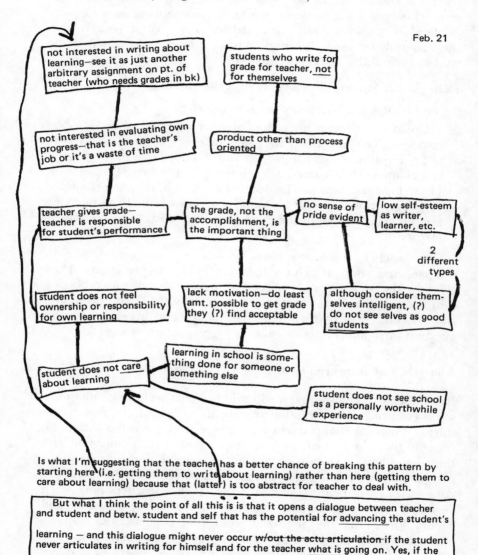

Feb. 21

not interested in writing about learning—see it as just another arbitrary assignment on pt. of teacher (who needs grades in bk)

students who write for grade for teacher, not for themselves

not interested in evaluating own progress—that is the teacher's job or it's a waste of time

product other than process oriented

teacher gives grade—teacher is responsible for student's performance

the grade, not the accomplishment, is the important thing

no sense of pride evident

low self-esteem as writer, learner, etc.

2 different types

student does not feel ownership or responsibility for own learning

lack motivation—do least amt. possible to get grade they (?) find acceptable

although consider themselves intelligent, (?) do not see selves as good students

learning in school is something done for someone or something else

student does not care about learning

student does not see school as a personally worthwhile experience

Is what I'm suggesting that the teacher has a better chance of breaking this pattern by starting here (i.e. getting them to write about learning) rather than here (getting them to care about learning) because that (latter) is too abstract for teacher to deal with.

But what I think the point of all this is is that it opens a dialogue between teacher and student and betw. student and self that has the potential for advancing the student's

learning — and this dialogue might never occur w/out the actu articulation if the student never articulates in writing for himself and for the teacher what is going on. Yes, if the

student and the teacher remain focused only on the pr end product of the process, neither will learn much from or about the process itself.

(From Patty Sue Williams's data, 1981–82)
3/10/83: 4:00 a.m.

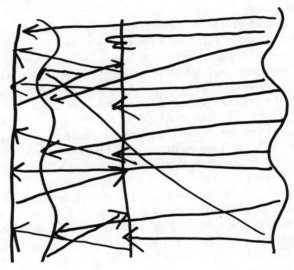

```
                                    3 / 10 / 83
                                    4: A.M.

        I threw away the "key", but the "tunnel" image kept
    nagging me.  I think the solution is that there is not
    "a" conection connection but "connections."

    _____ has been able to make several different kinds
    of connections between her reading process and her
    writing process, connections at different "doors."

            develop stages

            Reading            Writing        Environment
            Process            Process
```

This diagram
could be the
explanation of
how it happens.

I think I need to
fill it in more
  formally.

We think it is important for teachers to make up their own charts, pictures, lists, and systems since the frameworks for seeing the context offer information about the context. A physics teacher, therefore, may seek to understand what happens in learning logs in terms of problem solving; a first-grade teacher may see beginning writers' work in terms of repetitions. When teacher-researchers do attempt to use the taxonomies or schemata of other researchers in their fields, they tend to address those systems only to leave them behind as they go on to frame their own, which are more applicable to the contexts of their research. If they quantify some of their data (survey results, for example), they may use their quantifications to inform their overall analysis at this point.

During analysis, the small group is essential in helping teacher-researchers see patterns, in developing a focus, and in organizing principles of the research. Rereading the log entries, asking more questions of their students, and conducting follow-up interviews all characterize this stage of analysis. Continuing to write in a constant attempt to understand what the data reveal is also important to the teacher-researchers. As analysis continues, new teaching strategies are developed, tried, and woven into the pattern. Some teachers arrive at a more analytical understanding of their work in their final reports than others do, but all move analytically toward the non-judgmental stance, questioning their fundamental assumptions about teaching and learning.

In analyzing, teacher-researchers look for surprises, the unexpected events. As they formulate possible explanations for what they see happening in their classrooms, they apply their understanding to what they see, but when something happens that contradicts their expectations, they struggle to uncover the underlying principle that makes the occurrence of two seemingly contradictory events happen. For example, if most competent revisers in the class revise larger issues in their pieces before smaller questions of mechanics, but one student (also a competent reviser) always corrects spelling mistakes first, what is the underlying principle that unites the two seemingly contradictory events?

Analysis of the kind we are describing leads teachers to observe and analyze their own practices and, by looking at inconsistencies, learn more about what they do and why. These inconsistencies are informative, much like "errors" in a student paper. Uncovering them helps teachers work toward the integration of their practices and their theories.

A difficulty of this kind of analysis is the desire to have the emerging understanding be both accurate and tidy. The urge is particularly strong as the final drafts of the reports are written—drafts that are very much a part of the analysis itself. Honesty and the acknowledgment that the picture is not completely rosy characterize the research process and its results.

Example 14: An Unrosy Picture

(From the log of Judy Grumbacher, high school physics teacher, 1984–85)

1:20 (6th period)

A small revolt—I'd forgotten I told 6th period the quiz would be Tuesday—because I'd missed 6th period more last week than my other classes. So we're using the quiz as practice and I'll have to write a new quiz tonight. And badger the Xeroxer to run it off tomorrow. While the kids work, it gives me a chance to continue thinking about vectors. The kids need some understanding of vector quantities in order to understand how friction opposes motion and how momentum is conserved in collisions. It is also necessary to understand how projectiles move and why buildings don't (or occasionally do) fall down. I think those are reasonably important things to know. What I need to do, it is clear, is rethink the way I'm presenting this stuff. The Piagetians say that we fall back to lower developmental stages when we are presented with new unfamiliar stuff. Maybe we need some concrete experience. It occurs to me that I need to hand out the long tape measure and force balances and take the kids out to the hockey field to play vectors. That sounds like a lesson plan—now if it just doesn't rain tomorrow.

I've been thinking about arranging the kids into study groups. Maybe that's what I need to do, also. (I remember reading an article about some screen writers—they said "everything is copy." Sometimes I feel as if the corollary to that is "everything is research.")

With vectors I've not been able to relate the work well to the logs. The kids either aren't writing about vectors or they don't see the point. Something isn't right here.

Oct. 31, 1984: 11:00 a.m.

A second try at getting vectors right! Yesterday we spent a lot of time talking about what vectors are good for. I'd done this before, but the message hadn't gotten through. I still think a lot of kids think that when the new quarter begins next week, vectors will magically disappear. They won't. I've done as much with them (vectors and kids, too, I guess) as I can at this time. If I have to I'll reteach (not that I've taught them really yet) vector stuff when we get to momentum. Any more time on this stuff now is just spinning wheels and getting deeper and deeper in the mud.

I'm teaching a new course and new text with my GT [Gifted and Talented] class this year. And I'm presenting some topics I haven't worked with in a long time and that I've never taught before. I was having trouble explaining to a kid how forces act through a hinged joint. I knew I had to do a better job than I'd done—simply saying "forces can act in any direction through a hinge" didn't help the kid. I suspect that others in class wondered about this also, but didn't want to ask. Many of my GT kids just write down everything I put on the board and assume it's right— a bad assumption since I've been making mistakes right and left recently when I solve problems on the board.

Back to the hinges—so I sat down yesterday during 6th period— while the class was taking a quiz—and *wrote* about what I needed to clear up in class today. As I was writing I thought of a bunch of examples to use about how force acts through a hinge. I think those examples will help. Now it all seems so clear—how to present the hinge problem—I need to start by talking about—demonstrating is even better—the handle on a lawn mower. As the angle changes, so does the effective force—this is an example more kids are familiar with than the boom crane I started with. Writing to learn how to teach!

(I'm sorry now I didn't write all that stuff about hinges and cranes in my log . . . I'm getting as careless as my students . . .)

Example 15: Teacher-Researchers' Descriptions of Their Research Processes

(From Marion MacLean's work, 1981–82)

An Outline of a Teacher-Researcher's Process after the Fact

September 10: In-class reaction writing to first half of *Oedipus Rex.*

September 11: In-class reaction writing to the whole play.

September 14: Think-writings on articles about *Oedipus Rex* reveal that many of my students are writing to me. We discuss audience and writing to ourselves.

September 16: I assign a think-writing (on the *Poetics*) that I do not collect.

September 29– October 2: Conferences on *Oedipus* papers.

September 30: First teacher-researcher class meeting.

*October 8: During the essay test on *Oedipus* I try a lengthy, detailed observation of one student.

*October 13: After a couple of days of personal writing ("When I was a kid . . ."), I ask my students to write down their reactions to writing personally and any reasons for their not wanting me to

read what they had written (a few have expressed reservations in class).

October 14: More personal writing in class after which I read what I have written. Research class meets.

*October 15: I ask them to write a description of the audience to whom they imagine they are writing their college application essays.

*October 19: Taped interview with one student about his college application essay.

*October 20: Taped interview with Chris about his *Oedipus* and application essays.

*October 28: Research log entry on why I feel that I cannot grade papers any more. Research class meets.

*October 30: I ask my students (who are well into the writing of the application essay) to write out the story of writing that essay or to describe where they are at this point in shaping it into a final writing.

*November 7: I write out in my research log a conference with myself about the topic for my research. Later I will see that I am listening to an internal dialogue similar to ones that show up in my own students' comments on their papers.

*November 11: I ask my students to write out evaluations of their work for the first quarter. Research class meets.

November 23: My students meet in reading/writing groups for the first time. I write many observations about this and their subsequent group meetings in my log.

December 2: Research class meets.

December 7: I ask students at the end of the reading/writing group sessions to think about the criteria for evaluating writing: what criteria can we use to designate any writing as excellent?

*December 9: We discuss the criteria that they come up with in class. I then ask them to write their reactions to being evaluated by those criteria.

December 16: Research class meets.

*December 22: I ask one of the classes to write evaluations of themselves in their reading/writing groups.

January 6: Research class meets. My log reflects that I feel awash, uncertain, overwhelmed.

January 7: Discussion of evaluation of papers (I'm behind in evaluating theirs).

January 13: Their critical analysis papers are due; I have them write their own comments on their papers. (Major data source.) That afternoon I interview Chris again.

January 20: Research class meets. We attempt to write clearly limited research questions.

February 3: I ask my students to write out evaluations of their work for 2nd quarter. Research class meets.

February 8: I ask my students to write about the writing of their *Hamlet* papers.

February 10 & 11: I interview 6 students, ask questions about the comments they wrote on their papers on January 13, and encourage them to talk about their writing.

February-May: Six more research class meetings (most with research support groups); much rereading of data; attempts at analysis, drafts; students' reactions to drafts; revisions; pressure; publication). Paper due May 5th.

*Data collected, reread, transcribed, analyzed, and kept.

(From Carin Hauser, elementary school teacher, 1983-84)

The History of a Research Project	For Teacher-Researchers: Some Notes on the Process of Research

September

During the first seminar meeting, I reflected on what I was curious about in my writing program. What puzzled me? Intrigued me? Bothered me? My initial journal entry was: I am curious about young children revising. I'd like to know more about how they view revision and what reasons they have for doing it.

Start with a question about your students' learning or your teaching, something you *care* about, something that you want to clarify or understand.

Our research group met every other Thursday for two semesters. During the September meetings, my fellow researchers and I discussed articles we had read pertaining to the history of writing research and to its methodology. Cindi, Elly, and I formed a small group; this was the start of a very special collaborative relationship.

Meet with other teachers to discuss your research as you develop the study and collect your data.

In my own classroom, my students and I participated in a writers' workshop every day for almost an hour, as we did throughout the school year. I tried to record in my journal what I saw going on in our writers' workshops. I had a heightened awareness of the way children talked about their writing, and I tried to make notes on this "talk." Early in my study, I closely observed one child, Tara, while she wrote, and entered this information in my journal. I noted her pauses and rereading; all of these notes became helpful information later.

Keep a log; record observations and reflections on those observations; record your reactions to the process of your research study; raise new questions pertinent to your data.

October

During our teacher-researcher meetings, we continued to read and discuss articles about the methodology of teacher research, noting especially the nature of context-dependent studies. In the small group, Cindi, Elly, and I read portions of our journals to each other and helped each other begin to clarify where we were going with our research and how we would collect data. We each had intuitions about our general directions, but we had not focused our questions clearly, yet. The seminar leaders, Marian and Marion, provided us with useful, challenging responses to our written queries and entries. Informal chats with these veteran researchers also helped us over stuck points, steered us towards more productive routes of inquiry, and just plain encouraged us.

Read the reports of other teacher-researchers. Study the methodology behind their findings.

In my classroom, I interviewed all of the students, asking them to find their best piece of writing and to tell me why they thought these were their "best so far." I recorded each child's answer, analyzed (examined, compared, catego-

Establish a broad base for the collection of data. Document as fully as possible the context of your study.

rized) their responses, and coded them. I was surprised and a little disappointed with the results of this informal inventory. However, this was the beginning of a wonderful partnership between my students and me. As they watched me write down their responses in my journal, some of them even giggled. They saw that I was interested in what they said about their writing. At this point, I thought I'd study the evolution of writers' talk in our classroom. I had in mind some kind of "before and after" comparisons.

Follow your instincts.

During writers' workshop, students started talking about the changes they make on their drafts and about the problems they find and solve in their writing, as part of sharing time. I continued keeping "field notes" and started to tape some of the reading/ writing group conferences as part of the data I would need to analyze the writers' talk going on in the class. I saved most of the students' drafts, along with any revisions, in their writing folders.

Keep up your log throughout the entire study, even when you start to write your report.

Use several different means of collecting data in order to confirm the results of your analysis (triangulation of data).

November

Research seminar continued. In our small group, we shared journal entries and data we'd collected so far. We made attempts at refining our questions.

Clarify and refine your research question as you continue your study.

I started to focus my observations and note-making on Lindsay and Andrew, while noting the development and interactions of the other children. I examined closely the revisions Andrew and Lindsay made to their texts and taped a conference with Lindsay. Afterwards I made notes on her conference behaviors. In my journal, I started to question why Lindsay revised and to reexamine my own behaviors during the conference.

As nonjudgmentally as possible, consider your behaviors and interventions in the study.

December

Our seminars focused on analyzing data; we discussed model studies. The Estabrook article, "Talking about Writing: Developing Independent Writers," became an important article for me. In our small group, we attempted to clarify the contents of the "data packet" each of us was assembling. We made further attempts at clarification of our research questions. Each of us began to focus our attention on a smaller portion of our original student group.

I asked each child to answer a questionnaire: What makes you feel like a writer? What is your best piece of writing? Why? What would you like to change about the writers' workshop? In order to start the analysis of my project, I compiled a data packet, which included key drafts from Andrew and Lindsay, journal notes, and notes on the conferences. The journal notes already contained some analysis of the conference behaviors (both students' and mine). In my journal, I tried to make sense of the observations I had recorded. I kept trying to focus my question.

Make an attempt to define a reasonable time frame for collection of data. Start serious analysis of what you have found. Share your tentative findings with other teachers. Ask for feedback.

If you are concentrating on a small portion of your class (such as in a case study), continue to note the interactions of the children in the larger group.

Continue to refine your question. Look for emerging patterns in your data.

January

I asked Andrew and Lindsay to choose their three best writings and to examine any changes they had made to their first drafts. In the margin of each story, they wrote about their reasons for the changes. I then taped interviews with Andrew and Lindsay about these three "best" pieces. I also taped a revision conference with each of them.

In an exploratory draft, I tried to write about Andrew's and Lindsay's development as revisers over the course of

Take a break from pondering the meaning of your research.

Ask yourself: What do I still need to know?

After the exploratory draft, ask again, what do I still need to find out?

the first four months of school. I scru-
tinized their writings, the taped conferences, and the interviews, as well as my
journal. I was surprised at what happens
when you examine a small packet of
data intensely. I began to suspect that I
didn't have as much data on Andrew's
development as I did on Lindsay's development as a reviser.

In analyzing the tapes and notes, I realized that Lindsay's behaviors during
the conferences had changed, opening
up a new avenue of thought. I found
myself wondering about the structure
of the conference and how that structure
influenced revisions.

February–April

We had an unusual assignment. We were
to draw a picture of our research. The
purpose was to help us see the connections between the different parts of our
research, to start to visualize our analysis. My picture resembled a web of
ideas. The exercise forced me to see
connections: the students' revisions and
intuition, our writing conferences, and
the classroom's workshop environment
emerged as the key components of the
study. We researchers then wrote our
first drafts. During the writing, I realized
that I did not have enough information
about Andrew's process of writing. I
decided to pursue only Lindsay's development and save the data on Andrew
for another study.

The small groups were extremely helpful during the writing of many drafts
and the difficult task of analyzing what
was happening in the data. At different
points during the writing of the research, Cindi and Elly urged me to go

Analyze your data. What
are the patterns you see
reflected by the data? Strive
for objectivity. (This is
hard!)

Attempt to find new mean-
ings *as* you write your report. Go back to your data.

Share your drafts of your
report with other teachers.
Share your drafts with your
students too.

back to Lindsay and find out more information, to consider my role objec-
tively, and to describe further what was
going on in the rest of the class to make
the picture more realistic. In early April,
I conducted a follow-up interview with
Lindsay. The findings surprised me,
showing that her concept of revision was
continuing to evolve as she became a
more experienced writer and as she ma-
tured. The writing of the report was a
very messy event, resulting in two final
drafts and about four distinct and very
different in-between drafts.

May

Group publication and dinner party.

Share your findings with
other teachers. Pose new
questions.

Implications

At first, teachers may worry that as researchers they will have to
observe what happens in their classes without intervening. As they
continue, they realize that their interventions are at the heart of the
research, a part of what they are documenting and describing. They
observe themselves as well as their students. Their actions and the
students' subsequent reactions are important to their research findings. The story of how their research evolves is a vital part of their
research report.

Ordinarily, a teacher tries a lesson, notices how it goes, decides
whether or not it works, and then either throws away the plans or
files them for future use. When conducting research, the teacher
studies the teaching process and the students' reactions, collects a
variety of data, analyzes this information, organizes it into findings,
and considers the findings' implications for teaching. This process
sees daily lessons as part of a much larger picture and enables a
teacher to interrelate practices and theories that take many variables
into account.

Example 16: Research and Lesson Plans

(From the log of Leslie Gray, high school social studies teacher, 1984–85)

9/13/84: in class

I'm curious about concept development and how that can be enhanced by writing. When the kids did those dynamite synectic writings the other day did it enhance their understanding of the concept of immigration? I'm still a beginner at leading them in this type of writing, but does it have value beyond "sounding dynamite"? What happens to their ability to understand a unit conceptually?

I'm also curious about their current events logs. What happens when they write for an audience in the future about how they see their world today? Will they see the past differently if they are writing a "primary source"? Will they care about the present more?

9/14: in my classroom/free period

The current events log is changing the way I teach. I'm using it to introduce the unit on Labor Unions. I'm going to have them look at that picture of the coal mining boys on p. 273 and answer these questions: What questions would you ask them? What would you want to know about their jobs? their lives? the way their jobs affected their lives? For this log they will write about *their* jobs for a future audience. As a result, will they care more about those boys? Will they think more about work and its place in American society? Or consider its priority and place in their lives?

I think I'll have them hand in a piece of historical evidence with this one. By gathering evidence from around them and deciding why it is significant they'll learn how to be object literate and document literate. This log needs to come to life, so I will encourage them to find a picture of the personality they wrote about last week. Maybe that will bring some voices into their writing.

After 3rd period

We listed questions on the board they would ask the boys in the picture if they could. That activity was the prewriting for this log. These prewriting sessions on the log are worth examining. Instead of taking time *from* instruction they have *become* instruction.

During the explanation of the log writing on personalities, I explained the categories a historian looks at when studying history. The log has been a vehicle for removing the emphasis on political history that makes high school history so deadly dull. I'm feeling freed up by this too—freer to spend time on things other than political history, such as linear, chronological history.

What are we doing here? What happened in my class today?

1. Motivation—They are now interested in the plight of the working class in the late nineteenth century.
2. They are becoming document literate. By attaching some "thing" from their workplace to their entry, they are seeing how historians can use documents to study the past.
3. They are relating the past to the present, sensing the similarities and differences.
4. They are relating the present to the future—seeing their lives and their jobs as being historical fodder for the future.

After 6th period

Another dimension grew as the lesson was completed during fifth and sixth hours: After listing on the board the questions they would ask (15–20 in all), I asked for a show of hands regarding how many of them have worked in a fast food restaurant. Then, I asked those students the same questions that were on the board. I think the kids felt the link-*I* sure did. Sample questions:

How do you feel when you get off work?

Do you have to work?

What are your wages? Are they worth the work required?

Could you have a different job?

Would you rather go to school?

Did you every have any fun times on the job?

Teacher-researchers teach within a theoretical framework that, at the same time, they constantly observe, document, and revise. In this way, they integrate theory and practice. A self-sufficient lesson-plan or pass-the-time approach to teaching does not allow for or encourage integration of the teaching process. Teacher-researchers may begin to see themselves as responsible for acquiring and integrating new teaching practices and theories, thereby conducting their own "inservices." They document the process of learning to teach.

Most teacher-researcher articles are primarily about teacher change and how it occurred. They also discuss student change and what the teacher did to encourage it. The articles are filled with wonderful hints about classroom management and lesson planning, but they don't stop there. They go beyond classroom mechanics to offer fundamental hypotheses about teaching and learning. Nearly every teacher-researcher notes that it is his or her demonstrating the behavior of a researcher, a learner, a questioner, and a writer that really teaches the students how to learn. Taken as a whole, the articles have significant implications for curriculum and for teacher training.

For many years, there has been a tradition of "action research" that has gained or lost popularity depending on teacher autonomy. This kind of research, actively pursued in Great Britain (Nixon 1981), is taken on and written about in terms of curriculum. The research we are describing may or may not lead to curriculum change, because it is directed to other teachers. That is not to say that it has no implications for curriculum. In fact, the findings may go beyond the classroom curriculum to question the district's curriculum. In some cases the teacher-researcher may also see implications for the larger educational community, as in the case of a first-grade teacher's examination of basal readers and how they affect students learning to read and write.

Although the teachers themselves do not include this area in their articles, we think that their work, seen as a whole, has implications for inservice and preservice training. After encountering the methodology and the process used by teacher-researchers, teachers develop a kind of self-originated inservice that allows them to grow and to change as they work, contributing their much-needed ideas about learning and teaching to the profession.

Research Reports and Group Publication

We believe that it is very important to bring a teacher-researcher's study to a conclusion, however tentative the findings are and however clear it is that the study will continue. Rare is the teacher who is able, without the pressure of colleagues and deadlines, to write and publish for his or her own satisfaction. Teachers of grades K–12 find little encouragement for personal contemplation and writing during their school day. Therefore, we believe it is important for the teacher-reseachers to produce a modest group publication by a determined deadline.

In our groups, the reports have taken one of three forms. The I-Search paper, patterned after Ken Macrorie's description in *Searching Writing*, is probably the most common. Teachers who have used their studies to explore their own teaching document their changes as teachers as frequently as (and sometimes more often than) they document the changes of their students. They may also document what they learned from their students as they began to regard their classroom as a place to conduct research.

The next most common form of the research report is an article focusing on a research question or questions, an explanation of data collection procedures, or an analysis and interpretation of the data, the findings, and the implications of the findings for teaching. Although these articles explain in detail the teacher's role in the study, they focus less on the teacher and more on what has happened to the students: how students have changed or not changed, what students say about what has happened, and what teachers observe about the students' work and behavior.

The research proposal is the most infrequently used form of the research reports. Sometimes the proposal is written to an (as yet) unknown audience, but several of the teachers in the course have used this study to prepare them for a master's thesis or for doctoral work. In some cases, we believe, the research has been the impetus the teacher needed to continue studies at a higher level. The proposals are usually written in a conventional format and refer to the current preliminary study and its outcomes as the source of hypotheses for future work. (For a sample proposal format, see Appendix C.)

Most of the reports require the maximum length of ten pages, a limit originally intended to minimize the costs of copying the group publication. The length is compatible with articles appearing in publications like *English Journal* and *Language Arts*, and many of the articles from the classes have been published in these journals.

The deadline drafts of these writings for the group publication are important for closure on the process of researching. Without them, many teacher-researchers could go on happily collecting data without every approaching analysis, just as many have collected lesson plans and handouts from other teachers in an effort to add grounding to their teaching. Writing the report gives them a sense of knowing, "Here is where I am now, this is what I think now, and these are the questions I still have."

The teacher-researchers write first for themselves, next for each other, and finally for the professional community in general. The writing process introduces many to the wide professional arena that is the context for the discussion of many of the issues they raise.

Issues and Complexities

"All the classes I've attended (and taught), all the curriculum guides I've followed, all the lesson plans I've written, and all the texts I've read really didn't mean anything to *me personally* until I became a teacher-researcher."

Teacher-Researcher Role Tension

Research that teachers conduct in their own classrooms differs significantly both from ethnographical and educational research that is experimental in design. Ethnographers are new to and separate from the situations they enter. For them, the distance is the starting point. Their problem is gaining entry to the group, establishing and maintaining trust, and then dealing with the role tension that arises out of being both participant and observer. Teacher-researchers deal with the same participant-observer role tension, but for them the starting point is one of participation, not observation—immersion, not distance. Distance is for teacher-researchers the ultimately unachievable condition, just as participation is for an ethnographer. A teacher-researcher's problem arises out of the effort to become an observer with a nonjudgmental, distanced viewpoint.

The shift in stance that is difficult for a teacher-researcher is not a shift away from being a teacher toward being a researcher. It is more a move away from being only a participant, even a thoughtful and conscientious one, toward being someone who has the distance to examine the participant role. The difficulty lies in becoming not teachers or researchers, but both.

Teacher-researchers may experience conflict as they come to see their students' work differently. Homework becomes more than just papers to grade; it is now part of their data, a key to understanding what their students may be learning and what direction their instruction should take. A teacher may receive a set of papers and look

55

through them only to discover how little the students have done to meet the teacher's expectations. The teacher may well feel disappointed. As a researcher, however, the teacher may find it helpful to try to understand what these students' papers indicate about what has happened. The students' papers have become informative data that may disclose principles and assumptions at work in the classroom of which the teachers were unaware. With the distance that the researcher's stance offers, student work becomes interesting and informative—no matter what level of performance or quality of work was done.

Under these circumstances, both the teacher-researcher and the students can look at the class work to determine logically what step should come next. The students share the responsibility for their learning with their teacher rather than assuming a more traditional passive role. Rather than making value judgments on students' work, the teacher-researcher tries to discover what happens when students make errors or experiment with writing. Student errors, when they become a part of research, take on a different aura. They are the points of change, informative shifts, and are of interest to both student and teacher. Student errors are not something that needs to be punished or hidden. Instead, they should be recognized as important clues to the learning process.

Assumptions of Authority

In ethnography, the researcher's established first role is that of observer and outsider; for a teacher, the first established role is that of authority in the classroom. For the teacher-researcher, this authority can be one of the first major assumptions that comes into question.

Imagine the situations that arise. Students are trying to write journal entries at the beginning of the class period. Jeff, a student who has been disrupting class frequently enough to get on everyone's nerves, is staring at his paper and drumming his pen more and more loudly against the metal base of his desk. The teacher is a researcher whose job is to observe, describe, and reflect on what is happening in the classroom: to question, not to make assumptions. In the research log, the researcher writes observations of Jeff's behavior and makes notes on reactions or lack of reactions by the rest of the class, perhaps even jotting down the "teacher's" reactions, too. Finally, the researcher makes a note to ask Jeff a question later that will lead to understanding the function of his pen-tapping during that day's journal writing.

But the researcher is also the teacher. The person in this role has a responsibility to make the classroom an environment in which everyone can work, assuming that reducing the distractions will help people work. The teacher wants Jeff to be quiet and to get his writing done. Even though the teacher may wonder why Jeff isn't writing, the teacher's responsibility seems clear.

Most teacher-researchers experience this conflict. For many, it raises issues of authority and control that produce conflicting reactions. Those who, despite their uneasiness, investigate these issues with their students note that classroom management and discipline become less problematic and more integrated with learning.

Teachers and students live and work together daily, assuming certain ground rules. As a teacher enters into research, he or she calls those ground rules into question. The teacher may first surprise the students by asking them a question to which they know the answer and the teacher doesn't. Then the teacher surprises them again, and they start to surprise each other as they look together at the ground rules that all of them once just obeyed without noticing. It makes everyone a little nervous and a little excited at the same time because it seems clear that they are all suddenly on different ground, looking at the same things and helping each other to see.

Example 17: Teacher-Researchers Learning from Their Students

(From the log and data of Lin McKay, high school English teacher, 1984–85)
Reflections: 11/8/84

Since I'm tempted to try to write the story of what's happening now as I have begun the research in class, I'm interested in knowing what's happening to the kids as we embark together. Hence, the question I posed to them: "What happens to you when you're aware that I'm observing and recording the actions of the class as you all write?" I'm interested not only in the story of my question, "What happens when students make observations about their writing?", but also in the story of the research experience itself. I've received some interesting observations I've attached.

I hadn't told them yet about the bond I've been feeling with them, but I will. And I'm curious about their experience. Some students' comments:

When I'm writing and get observed, it doesn't really distract me but encourages me. It lets me know that I should be writing, nothing else. I feel better, for some reason knowing that everyone else is doing the same thing.

When Mrs. McKay is watching me write, a question appears in my mind. "What am I doing to attract this attention?" It must be she likes young minds to think and express their ideas. I'm not afraid of this stare but I still wonder.

When you're observing us write I really don't notice and I think I write pretty much the same. But I'm glad you're observing us. It makes me feel more important, like my writings mean something. So in a real sense I'm very glad you're observing us. I guess it kind of puts me at ease.

I really don't really feel anything when you're observing us. I get involved in what I'm writing and I can't concentrate on two different things going on at the same time, so I just write and not worry about anything else.

I really don't mind when you observe me writing. In fact, half the time I don't even notice and the other half I kind of like it because I hope you'll write down something about "Karen's unique ways of writing." I think it would be neat to be used in one of your seminar thingys, so no I don't mind it when you observe me, as long as you observe quietly!

When you observe us—this may sound stuck up—I feel like I need to put on a show. This probably doesn't do anything for your study but I can't help it. I feel like I really want to be a part of something. Even a stupid survey. When I concentrate sometimes I lick my lips, so when I think you're watching I overdo it. Sound stupid?! Admitting it like this makes me feel dumb.

I really don't pay much attention to what you are doing while I am writing. I try to devote all of my attention and concentration to the writing at hand. I do appreciate, however, the fact that you are paying attention to what we are doing and are taking the time to analyze and try to make better our writing habits. Because of the huge amount of writing that we have done I do feel that my writing is much more fluent. I find it much easier to write.

I feel privileged that I am part of this project and it makes me feel special. At first I didn't know what to think and felt a little nervous, but I'm not anymore. I feel that it is also helping me in my writings also.

> Until now I have been faintly aware that you have been "watching" us. But even though you have been watching us, it really does not make any difference to me. I think the reason it does not bother me is because when I write, I don't look at you, I look at my paper.

Many teacher-researchers make repeated references to learning from their students, learning that is documented in their research. In fact, the success of their research depends to some extent on this learning, because their students are their subjects—not in the sense of a kingdom, not even in the sense of a psychology laboratory, but in the sense that they are what the teacher goes to school to learn about.

Most teacher-researchers find this part of the work and its collaborative nature exciting and somewhat different from the ways they have worked with students previously. But then the period of analysis arrives along with the necessity of revising some of their assumptions— this time to achieve authority over their data and to interpret their experience. During data collection, they have been learning the value of each individual's authority and control. But both the analysis of data and the writing of the final report require that they establish authority over their own material, an authority derived from their own understanding of what has happened. Although teacher-researchers find it difficult to write with a sense of authority when questioning that quality in their research, the writing that results is often more powerful as a result of their struggle.

Example 18: A Teacher-Researcher on the Issue of Her Own Authority

(From Patty Sue Williams's log, 1982–83)
2/6/83

> I am also becoming aware of when I can really create and when I'm just writing to be putting words on paper. My writing reflects my voice more and more and it's not a weak voice. I think there was a time when I delayed writing because I feared having a weak, nonauthoritative voice. I think Kim [the student in Williams's case study] discovered her voice before I did. I think my "specialty" is being able to look at the children's writing and discover each one's uniqueness, examining their writing processes and seeing myself mirrored there.

Example 19: A Teacher-Researcher Examines the Issue of Authority
during the Research Process

(From an article by Gloria Johnson, high school English teacher,
1981–82)

During the year our roles became more refined. I became a
facilitator, a partner striving to create a positive environment for
individuals and for the class as an entity. Every day I tried to create
an atmosphere in which every student was accepted, was important,
was equal, was listened to, and was valued. We took notes a lot
and laughed a lot with each other. We were comfortable; we liked
each other; and we learned a lot. Endlessly, I encouraged and tried
to teach the importance of self-evaluation. The students became
authors. We had great respect for each others' roles and for each
other as individuals. . . .

The students chose their seats, offered significant input into
their group assignment, became increasingly involved in class
discussions about their writing, selected their own topics, helped
determine assignments, and evaluated themselves. They felt comfortable disagreeing with me, and I did not feel threatened as I
listened, reevaluating my views often. Initially, I was their partner,
but they "bought out" my interests until they truly owned the end
products that emerged naturally and beautifully; however, most
important, they owned the process.

Finally, my increased awareness has altered my perception of
my role as a teacher of writing. I feel more and more important
in the directional process, not in the evaluative process. Together,
students and a teacher can discover and enjoy writing. While I
observed my students beginning to own their writing, I began to
own my teaching. What a marvelous feeling!

The Difficulty of Necessary Retreating

Even without the additional strains of conducting research in their
own classrooms, teachers have a difficult job. The constant interaction
with students, the pressures of the daily schedule, the desire that
students learn, and the need to live up to their own expectations all
contribute to the roles they assume and the decisions they make
about how to teach. They have to forget what teaching is like, we
believe, in order to be able to go back to it after a summer vacation,
a spring break, or even a weekend.

As teacher-researchers, teachers face what they do; the research makes teaching more difficult to "forget." Teacher-researchers talk about what happens in their classrooms. They write down what they see happening. They read narratives, descriptions, and observations—honest reports of their daily classroom lives—to other teachers. They submit portions of their lives to analysis, revealing themselves to others by writing for publication. Those aspects of teaching that teachers ordinarily view as private, teacher-researchers hold in front of themselves continually.

Example 20: A Teacher-Researcher Describes the Difficulty of Self-Examination

(From the log of Barbara Falcone, middle school English teacher, 1981–82)

I feel like a yo-yo. High hopes one day, dashed down the next! So much for my high hopes. These kids really make it tough to be optimistic. Perhaps I take things too seriously, but I believe their doing well in school is serious business.

After roll call I was not allowed to go over yesterday's classwork. They are so rude and disrespectful. I cannot tolerate it and it really hurts my feelings. I want *so much*, more than anything else in the world, to teach them. And *they won't let me.* . . .

A. keeps talking back to me. Her whining infuriates me. . . .

This class in reading/writing groups is a farce—Maybe I should drop it. They'll write "good," "nice," "great" on each other's papers, no matter how poorly or how well (a rarity) they are written.

As a group, they've just not "caught on" to the process yet, but I'm determined to hang in there. . . .

I asked Leila what she was doing and she replied, "Nothing." I praised her honesty.

(From Barbara Falcone's article, 1981–82)

My daily log of observations and reflections proved to be most beneficial because it offered me an opportunity to study the psychological interaction of teacher, student, and environment. It was good therapy, an "acceptable" release for my tension; it was a consistent record of both "good" and "bad" days that enabled me to look for patterns of behavior (with classes and individuals);

it helped me maintain my objectivity, to step back and not take the students' behavior so personally, giving me a perspective I needed when I felt too close to a problem; it provided insights for my teaching, theories, and intuitions, and gave me a deeper understanding of what was happening in the classroom; and it had a calming influence on the students whenever I wrote log entries *in class.*

Being a teacher-researcher made me more observant in the classroom and thus improved my teaching. It allowed me to offer support but simultaneously maintain a "distance." This turned out to be a good cure for my lagging dedication, more popularly referred to as "burn-out." I still cared—very much so—but part of me was able to step back and look at what I was doing or what the students were doing. Keeping the log forced me to think about what was happening every day. What is unique about that revelation? The answer is simply "Nothing." It is something I had to learn for myself by doing it. All the classes I've attended (and taught), all the curriculum guides I've followed, all the lesson plans I've written, and all the texts I've read really didn't mean anything to *me personally* until I became a teacher-researcher.

Teacher-researchers begin with what is already familiar to them— their students and their classrooms. As a result, it is difficult to gain distance and perspective, but, by doing so, they accomplish something even more difficult: they begin to examine themselves as part of the context. This examination, we think, is a fundamental characteristic of teacher-researchers: their research includes them as significant factors. They observe from an involved distance. Self-observation becomes a habit that provides its own reward. Teachers may (even if temporarily) see and think differently about themselves in their professional roles. They may also change the way they teach.

Validity and Reliability

Teacher-researchers, like all researchers, are concerned with the validity and reliability of their research. The extent to which they achieve these qualities varies as much as it does for other researchers, regardless of methodologies, goals, and theoretical frameworks.

At the beginning of their work, teacher-researchers may feel apprehensive about the value of the studies that they conduct in their own classrooms. As they observe and reflect, their questions about the value of their studies in a broader context usually diminish. They work hard to ensure the internal validity of their research because their studies become significant to them.

Teacher-researchers try to describe as accurately as possible the qualities of their teaching contexts and their research methods and processes. Because they are sensitive to the context-dependent nature of their work—and of all educational research—they produce research with a strong sense of the need to document context. Their insights gain validity through the honesty and rigor of their questions, their analyses, and their acknowledgment of what happens as they teach.

Alone, or in a different research setting, teacher-researchers might confront issues less, ignore disquieting data, or force findings. But we believe that the following characteristics of teacher-researcher groups promote the validity of their studies:

1. the frequency and consistency of observations

2. the reflections on and interpretations of data

3. a broad database from which to choose a specific focus

4. the careful scrutiny of other teacher-researchers who challenge the analysis and interpretation of the teacher-researcher

5. the variety of data that is collected

6. the triangulation of findings

7. the review of research findings by students, leaders, and peers

8. the use of readings from theoretical and methodological frameworks

Teacher-researchers' studies may have validity and produce reliable insights and findings with relatively little concern for replicability. One teacher-researcher may document complex critical thinking in a group of first graders. That study may not be exactly replicable, but it documents a finding that is valid for and reliable in one context—a finding that no subsequent study can ignore.

Teachers are sometimes understandably suspicious of educational research that claims reliability in classroom settings. They are well aware that no collection of fifteen-year-olds could be exactly replicated, that no one correct view exists of their management of classroom interruptions, and that the usefulness of some research methods can vary with time, group, and teacher. For these reasons, among others, teacher-researchers know that their own studies may not "translate" intact to other settings involving teachers and students who have different histories and relationships with each other. Teacher-researchers come to expect that their findings and those of their colleagues will differ with each educational context. By examining these differences, they see more clearly what is occurring.

Eventually, the issue of reliability may be addressed best by analyzing collections of teacher-researchers' studies. We hope for this kind of analysis as groups of teacher-researchers proliferate and as the collections of their studies grow.

It is our belief that a kind of reliability exists in studies that are context-specific, like those of teacher-researchers. Teacher-researchers want others to understand their findings, and they assume that other teachers will decide for themselves the value of a study's implications. Insights, analytical schemata, and findings come from a teacher-researcher's individual application of research processes and methods. Because of its specific and individual nature, a study reveals as much about the researcher as it does about the research.

Through the specific nature of teacher-researchers' reports and the personal nature of their interpretations, other teachers and readers see the generalizable "truths" that can be reliably interpreted as applicable in their classrooms. No classroom setting with all its variables can be replicated or controlled, but with enough information and solid, explanatory analysis, readers may discover findings that do apply in their own work with their own students.

Conclusion

As we write, we wonder if this is the outline of a book that is not ready to be written. Our uneasiness comes from our awareness that in education there is a history of fads and the mistaken belief that the only thing that teachers want is "something to do on Monday morning." As teacher-researchers, we do not want our work to become a fad, to have research processes reduced to a product, or to have what happened to a few teachers become codified as a process that all should follow.

We have tried to answer requests from other teachers and leaders of teacher groups for information about how to set up a program for teacher-researchers. We want to help, and we think it is an exciting, rewarding endeavor that may assist teachers in attaining their rightful place in the educational community as people who make informed decisions about the conduct, content, and practice of the profession.

Although it is our experience that teacher-researchers engage in something important and exciting during their work, that they do look at themselves differently in their classrooms, and that many of them change the ways that they teach, we have only the most tentative of hypotheses about what happens. We ourselves are unable to draw conclusions until other teacher-leaders and teacher-researchers conduct their research. We envision a large collection of individual reports by and about teacher-researchers, a collection to add to the data about what happens when teachers conduct research in their own classrooms.

We hope that by setting forth on such an effort we may enable others to do so also. We encourage teachers to organize groups for research, we urge teacher-leaders and school systems to aid them in their efforts, and we offer our support through this guide.

Those who care about raising the standards of teaching must help provide teachers with the time to raise the standards of their profession themselves. It was always time that teacher-researchers wanted and never time that anyone seemed willing or able to give—time to advance the research, to work with other teachers, to write, to accommodate the kind of professional development that replenishes both our profession and us.

Research Reports from Group Publications

The articles included here as samples appear as they did in the group publications, except for minor changes. All were written by the teacher-researchers whose work appears as the examples in this guide. Their studies represent the variety of forms the reports may take and the range of grade levels and subject areas encompassed by the group.

"I Think It Has Something to Do with Our Minds": Using Synectics to Learn about History
Leslie A. Gray

> I saw myself driving down a long dusty path and wondering what was going on and what would happen next. I even said to myself it would have been pretty neat to live back then, not for a long time, just a visit; sort of like an angel bringing me back to the past to see what it was really like.
>
> It's like being in another place and time for a few minutes. You begin to form new ideas and pictures of what you are studying.

The opening quotations are not about science fiction, and the experience they are recounting did not take place in a time machine. They are what my eleventh-grade U.S. history students told me happens when we do synectic writings about history topics. They told me that and much more as we explored together what happens when a history class writes synectically.

Synectics is a process developed by William Gordon which, through the use of metaphor and personalizing, helps students think about a subject from new angles. I first stumbled onto the ideas of William Gordon in Bruce Joyce's book *Personal Models of Teaching*. It had been

67

on my "to read" list for about six months, and I checked it out of the professional library during a one-week inservice that Fairfax County had funded on encouraging teachers to teach higher up on Bloom's taxonomy. The model lesson I read showed how a creative writing teacher used synectics to develop a character for a short story. I was fascinated and immediately wondered how a synectic development of say, social Darwinism, might help my students understand that concept and its influence in the post–Civil War era.

But there is a big leap from a flash of insight in an August inservice to implementing the idea into an already crowded curriculum. I decided to begin by integrating it into my first unit on post–Civil War America. One of my objectives in this unit is to have my students assess the treatment of racial and ethnic minorities by the majority in the North, South, and West. The immigrants from southern and eastern Europe were our first challenge. We had read primary and secondary source accounts and had gathered data on the experiences that different immigrant groups had as they came to America.

I was a little nervous that first day, so in preparation I read and reread the chapter in Joyce that divides the synectics process into six steps. I decided I could bite off three of those six steps my first time at bat. We would:

1. Define the problem: They would describe the experience of these immigrant groups by listing all they knew about such groups' experiences on the board.

2. Develop a direct analogy: They would choose a machine that is like the experience they had just described.

3. Develop a personal analogy: They would describe what it felt like to "be" that machine.

Having done all that, then we would write in our journals about the immigrant experience from the point of view of our analogy. By day's end, classes had compared the immigrant experience to a television, a slot machine, a log on a hydraulic log splitter, and a dishwasher.

> I'm a log being put through a hydraulic log splitter. Intense pressure is being forced onto me. I have no other choice except to continue in search of a better life. I'm being split in half, torn away from something important to me. After being separated from everything I have known, I wonder what will become of me. Will I contribute to the building of America and help this new country grow? Or will I be stacked up by the side of

the house, forgotten and miserable? Or perhaps I will not be able to adjust to the newness of my surroundings and perish in a fire? The uncertainty of the future is definitely frightening!

Leslie

I'm a machine that takes money. Travelers come. They want to play me. I give them a chance. Their odds are not good. They don't know what my owner does. He conceals the truth and the house makes more money. They occasionally win but not often enough. I just keep filling up with money for the house. The losers walk away . . . empty pockets . . . lost hope . . . lost dreams of riches. I know there will be another and another, because the house has misleading ads on every street corner, in every mailbox, on every doorstep. Come and play the slot machine. Go from rags to riches. But all I see is a trail of sad-faced losers who now understand my truth.

Doug

In her writing, Leslie focused on the feelings of uncertainty that these people must have felt, while Doug made a link to the misleading nature of the Horatio Alger image of the American Dream. I sensed that there was something to this process, but I was unsure of its value. Their writing was interesting, but this was, after all, a history class. What was happening to their understanding of the concept of immigration? Was this process worth a whole class period? I asked one of my colleagues to come in and take notes the next time I tried it. The account that follows is derived from the notes she took in my class.

This time I decided to add the final three steps that Gordon suggests.

4. Develop a compressed conflict: Students examine descriptions in steps 2 and 3 and suggest words that are in conflict.

5. Develop a new direct analogy: Students develop a new analogy based on the compressed conflict.

6. Reexamine the original task: Teacher gets students to move back to the original task and use the last analogy as a basis for a writing.

When the students arrived, all six steps were written across the top of the blackboard.

A Synectics Lesson

"O.K. Take out your journals. This is entry 7, 'Reconstruction and the Freedmen.' You all did such a great job on those slot machine writings, I thought we'd take it a step further today."

Using the notes they had taken previously, they described the situation of the freedmen. They all contributed as I wrote on the board and they copied the information into their journals.

Step 1: Define the problem

"They were free but not equal"... "harassed by the Klan"... "no political power"... "stuck by the state laws"... "only free as long as the Northern troops were there"... "hungry for an education"... "the promises of equality were broken in the Compromise of 1876."

Step 2: Develop a direct analogy

"Now look at the experience you've described," I directed. "Suppose I asked you to tell me something like what you see, only it's a machine."

We explored several possibilities and decided on a remote-control model airplane.

Step 3: Develop a personal analogy

"Now I'd like you to become that model airplane," I said. "What does it feel like?"

"I keep going around in circles, but I can't get anywhere." "I feel I have all kinds of potential to really fly, but I'm all hemmed in." "I get dizzy going around in circles." "I want to go higher, but I know I'm controlled by the guy with the remote-control unit."

Step 4: Develop a compressed conflict

"O.K.," I interjected, "let's take this a step further. Study what we have on the board under step 3. Look for contrasts. I want words or ideas from here that are in conflict."

leave/stuck
potential/restricted
free/control
moving/nowhere

"Which are most in conflict?"

They decide on free/control.

Step 5: Develop a new direct analogy

"Think about this idea of free/control. Could you give me an example from the animal world that has that idea in it?"

They shout out, "zoo," "animals in a cage," "fish in a tank," "horse in a corral," "carrier pigeon," and "falcon."

We choose fish in a tank, but some horse lovers decide to stay with horse in a corral.

"What does it feel like to be a fish in a tank?" I ask. "What do you see?"

"People outside the tank are bigger."

"You know those fake castles they have in the fish tanks?"

"The owner of the pet store controls my life. I have to depend on him for my food."

Step 6: Reexamine the original task

"O.K. I think we have enough. Now remember, our task is to describe what it was like to be a freedman after the Civil War. Let's write now about our topic as if we were a fish in a tank."

Prewriting as Learning

Before I share their samples, I think it's worthwhile to examine what has happened just in this prewriting phase. They have:

1. Recalled previous knowledge.
2. Applied that knowledge to a new understanding in trying to discover and decide on the best analogy.
3. Begun to enter into the feelings of people from the past.
4. Tentatively begun broadening their conceptual framework by testing whether the situations in their analogy have a counterpart in history.

All of those I can observe in the classroom give-and-take *before* we write. But what happens to their thinking and understanding as they create writings like the ones that follow?

> Have you ever lived in a closet that was locked and you could see through the cracks into the real world? Well that's what it's like for me. I am a goldfish in a huge fishtank cramped with many hundreds of other fish and for a very long time we were dependent on our owner for food, water, plants and all our necessities. But then all of a sudden we had our fish tank taken away and we were thrust into a loud, dirty, independent world

and we had to adapt to breathing air not water. The owners or ex-owners didn't like us and even though we were glad to be free of the tank we weren't sure if this was what we wanted for us and our children.

Dana

What a bum deal. I thought when he brought me out of that huge fish tank in the store I would be free. Not so. I am now in an even smaller tank and it's cramped. I don't like it here. It was almost better back in the store. This cage is too restricting. I need to be free. I don't like the environment. It is not what I wanted or expected. How can I tell him what I want? He is so big and I am so little. I need to be fed. I need my water changed. I need to be recognized as who I am. I am not just a dumb fish like everybody thinks. I am different. How can I tell him? I am restricted by my size and these walls. They are laughing at me. The walls know that they prevent me from being free and they are laughing. They love it. If I could only talk to him I could make him understand and see that I am me and not a toy or an ornament.

Rob

These two journal entries reflect that these students had come to a deeper understanding of "the facts" that had launched us off in step 1. *I* could see value in what they had done. I wondered if *they* could. In a move that was quite unplanned, I asked them to take out a fresh sheet of paper and answer the following question for me. "If people from another class asked you why we do these writings, what would you tell them?"

I am always amazed by what kids know, if only we'll ask them. This was one such occasion. As I sifted through their responses they seemed to fall into roughly four categories. They said that these writings helped them to

1. Connect things together

"It makes you put everything you learned together."

"It makes us think and building on an idea."

"We do these writings to help us get a clear idea of something that may not seem that clear to us. It's like a model that you can visualize which makes learning easier to do."

"To develop ideas that haven't surfaced and been put together in organized thinking yet."

"Sometimes complicated things are easier to understand when you relate them to real things that you know about."

2. Personalize their learning

"The writings, in my opinion, help us to find ourselves, to find out how we really think. But more importantly they help us to think and to feel. They make the subject we're dealing with so much more real and better understood."

"With these writings we can really speak our feelings. We can find a hole and channel *all* our thoughts and emotions through it. It makes it ten times easier to write when it is coming from our heart. We can formulate our opinions and be who we really are."

"It helps to tie in history with our reality and things start to make sense."

"It teaches us to relate all events in history with our life, so we can see how it all ties in. It makes history come to life and not sit in a book."

3. Experience the feelings of people in history

"You explore beyond the textbook and actually envision yourself experiencing the actual event. You wonder how the people felt and what they were actually thinking."

"I think we do these analogies because we can put ourselves in their shoes in history but base it on some object in today's time."

"Because we need to feel the way the people of history felt."

4. Think in new ways

"It is a different side of writing which we are not used to. It makes us think in a different way and use our brain differently."

" . . . gives us a chance to work our minds and think about the problem from different angles."

"To reach into the brain and getting what kind of imagination you have, because some people have imaginations, but don't show it."

"I think it has something to do with our minds."

There, in their own inimitable voices, was some fascinating data about the value of synectics in a history classroom. But I wanted to know more about the very act of writing. What went on inside their heads as they composed these writings? Since they had proven to be fairly articulate observers of their own processes in the past, I decided to use their own observations as a data source once again.

What Happens as They Write?

After completing a synectic writing on the decade of the 1920s, I asked my students to answer the question "What happened as you were writing that piece?" We had chosen as our analogy the idea of being a passenger in a car. Their responses to this question were not as easily given to categorization as they had been the last time. Some admitted that these writings "didn't work" for them.

Kurt, a good thinker and a straight-*A* student, talks about how it is difficult to personalize the analogy.

> For some reason I can't write these synectic writings. I can't become the thing I'm writing about. I'm not as creative as other people I guess. When I do this type of writing, it doesn't flow like the ones that people read aloud. I think I'm kind of intimidated by this different type of writing.
>
>   Kurt

I suspect there are others who don't reap the full benefit, and that those who admitted to it in their responses were more self-aware. Yet, clearly eighty percent did demonstrate in their response to this question that the writings were a benefit to their learning.

Phil, a reluctant user of his intellectual potential, shows in his response how important it is for him to relate history to something he knows about.

> I started out just following the directions and getting bored with it. Then I started to think of actual things that happened to me and write them down. I really got into it and it made it easier to write. I find it easier to write about things that I can relate to.
>
>   Phil

Kevin, who likes to write and for whom synectics comes easily, discovers in his writing an underlying tension of the 1920s.

> When I wrote that piece, I became a choice. I became a choice between old and new. The new was always unpredictable, but the old was always there to go back to. I felt that the future goal is the top of industry, or whatever would be the final result of one's progress. The writing better supported my understanding of the real question. The question of technology. I think that the question is whether technology is a bunch of worthless ideas or the key to the future.
>
>   Kevin

Trish discovered in her writing what history can tell us about our own lives.

> After writing this I know that the 1920s is a part of us. It's a little place in our own lives where we've got to grow up. It's like our nation was in the 1920s when they were children and

didn't want to grow up, but time caught up with them and changed them.

Trish

I present these merely as examples of ways some of them have used this process. Another day, another topic, and perhaps each would discover different insights or none at all. What is crucial here is that it is an opportunity for them to do what they're ready to do with the facts at hand. They are clearly dealing with the material higher up on Bloom's taxonomy than the level of memory recall.

Focusing on Debi's Process

Debi's responses and writings were typical of those of many students, so I decided to interview her. To her these writings were like a series of steps used in her mind to test the appropriateness of her analogy.

Step 1: "I try to think of some thing about the object, such as the passenger in the car has no control of the car."

Step 2: "Then I try to make it relate to our topic . . . the people in the '20s didn't try to control things like the economy."

Step 3: "If that fits, then I think about how the passenger would feel not to have any control. I might enjoy the lack of responsibility, sit back, watch things go by and have fun."

She is enthusiastic about this process, but admits she was skeptical at first.

> I'm the type who likes to read and answer questions. I learn better that way, so I didn't think this would help me much. But I find when we do these writings, I even do better on my objective tests. The metaphor becomes like the middle of the map and everything just falls into place. I still remember the Indian policy and the snowblower.

She reminded me that we had not done a synectic writing for our unit on World War I: "World War I is a big blank to me. I just couldn't get it together."

Synectic writing helped Debi place the facts in a conceptual framework. This framework helped her make meaning out of previously unconnected material. As she wrote she thought about an organizational framework and tested out her assumptions about their connectedness. Once in this conceptual framework, the knowledge stayed with her longer.

Findings and Conclusions

From my data I can conclude the following things. Writing synectically helps my students: think in new ways; personalize their learning; experience the feelings of people in the past; connect things together; develop a conceptual framework for a unit under study; recall objective material more easily; and remember material over time.

Questions for Further Study

Because it is linked with creativity, synectics has been a strategy associated with the gifted. My classes are not gifted and talented (GT) but are a heterogeneous grouping of all eleventh graders. I think more studies with a non-GT cohort would be of value to find out if it encourages higher-order thinking. Are average students who use synectics regularly better able to engage in higher-order skills such as analysis and synthesis?

Most students picked up this skill quickly. After four guided classroom sessions they were able to develop synectic writings in small groups, and some are quite capable of developing one independently. But I wonder about those for whom it does not work. Do these students have common characteristics? Is there a correlation between right brain/left brain function?

Implications

William Gordon developed synectics with the productive and creative potential of science and industry in mind—not my history classroom. But the concerns he writes about are in many ways concerns I have had as an educator. He believed that creativity was often "suffocated in the specialized semantics" of a particular discipline that tended to make reality abstract and secondhand (Gordon 1961). I know that over the years far too many of my students never cut through the secondhandedness of history. They got suffocated in events, people, and concepts they hadn't a clue of how to connect. To make his point Gordon quotes the English philosopher and mathematician Alfred North Whitehead, who observed that "the secondhandedness of the learned world is the secret of its mediocrity" (Gordon 1961). I believe that what Gordon hoped synectics would do for science and industry, it might also do for education.

The synectics process facilitates that very important element in learning that for want of a better word I would call "connecting." I have encountered this idea in several places over the last few years as I have become more familiar with the literature on writing and learning. In his book *Searching Writing*, Ken Macrorie talks of how real learning takes place on a Moebius Loop where the Self (my students) and the Others (U.S. history) flow into each other. If you run a pencil along the surface of a Moebius Loop, the line that starts on one side ends up on the surface of the other. If it is not a Moebius Loop, my students are stuck on the one side with no way to connect to my subject matter.

I've thought about that metaphor for a long time and wondered how often I have just put the Others out there without offering my students opportunities to connect to the Self. When I look at what my students told me in this study, I see them validating Macrorie's proposition. They said synectics helped them to "relate all events in history with our life," "put ourselves in their shoes," "find ourselves," "tie in history with our reality." They seemed to be saying that inviting the Self into the study of history is an important way to get to the Others. Or, put more directly, personalizing is not a luxury, it is a necessity to real learning.

References

Gordon, William J. J. 1961. *Synectics: The development of creative capacity*. New York: Harper & Row.
Joyce, B., M. Weil, and B. Kluwin. 1978. *Personal models of teaching*. Englewood Cliffs, N. J.: Prentice-Hall.
Macrorie, K. 1980. *Searching writing*. Rochelle Park, N. J.: Hayden Book Co.

What Happens When Mickey Writes? Reading between the Lines
Alberta N. Grossman

Mickey caught my attention early in the fall of his junior year at Glenville High School with the title and the message of his brief unsolicited essay:

> This Class Sucks
> I though this was go to be a class that help you work in other classes, not work in it. This class is boaing, dull. All we ever do is write write or write

"This Class . . ."came in response to my direction that students should develop one of the three ten-minute "freewritings" they had composed the previous week. Mickey had chosen a promising twenty-five-word (two-sentence) piece on climbing trees. But as soon as he sat down to write, he was overwhelmed with anger. The requirement was an assault.

Mickey represents a group of students for whom writing is more than the normal hard work that it is for the rest of us. Although his I.Q. is on the high side of average and his oral language is reasonably good, his written language is extremely limited. His spelling has the characteristic inconsistency of the learning-disabled (L.D.) writer. He spells a word as complicated as *neighborhood* correctly yet leaves off the "s" in *binoculars*, the "ed" in *landed*, and the "g" in *climbing*.

Even among learning-disabled writers, Mickey is seriously handicapped. For many L.D. writers, writing is not substantially more difficult than it is for other people once the requirement to spell and punctuate correctly is delayed until the end of the writing process. But although Mickey may be able to give a reasonably clear oral account of a personal experience, what he writes will be about one-half of what he can say. The language will be simpler and the ideas will be less complex. When Mickey writes about ideas and information he learns from books or discussion rather than from personal experience, he often leaves out much of what he has learned and asserts, "It makes perfect sense to me."

As Mickey began his eleventh-grade year at Glenville High School in September of 1980, he was handicapped in another way relative to the students in my Basic Skills class, a learning disabilities resource program. He had spent the previous five years in a self-contained program for learning-disabled students. In that program he had received all of his academic education from special education teachers. As an eleventh grader, he was joining the regular education program with only one period a day of L.D. resource support, against the advice of his L.D. teachers. They felt his skills, especially writing, and his ability to tolerate frustration, were too limited for success in the regular school program.

To me, "This Class . . ." was an acceptable way for Mickey to express his frustration. But his essay confirmed some of my doubts about the new writing techniques I was using. In September 1980, I had begun my ninth year of teaching, eager to apply the ideas about teaching writing I had learned that summer as a fellow of the Northern Virginia Writing Project. Already by the second week of school I could see that Mickey, along with the rest of my Basic Skills students, responded to some of these techniques. He loved the idea of brainstorming topics for writing. And although he didn't love writing for ten minutes on a topic he chose from the list, the Writing Project dictum "Write freely, don't worry about length, organization, or mechanics" at least got him to write. But even though these techniques worked, I had been concerned about how students like Mickey would respond when I asked them to develop and revise their writing. "This Class . . ." told me. Mickey anticipated pain, felt angry and defended himself by letting me know how he felt.

What follows is the chronicle of Mickey writing and not writing in the year and a half that I have known him. It is also the story of my attempts to cope with his pain and defenses.

September 1980–June 1981

Fortunately, in September of 1980, I didn't spend too much time wondering what my response should be to this boy who had such a good reason not to write. I decided to "tough it out." I said writing was an important part of the Basic Skills curriculum because it was important in all of his other classes. The dynamics of that class supported my stance. The students responded to the point system I had developed to encourage them to read their stories aloud, and Mickey, a natural storyteller, got caught up in the group spirit. After he wrote "This Class . . ." (to me) he told the rest of the "Trees" story to the group; then he wrote it down. Once he got the words on paper, however, he was not prepared to undertake any revision. On the next writing assignment, since I had identified "putting the words down on paper" as Mickey's chief writing problem, I suggested that he dictate his story to another student who typed as Mickey composed. The boy, a senior and a good listener, encouraged him to develop his stories.

In February 1981 I used Mickey's first story, "Trees," in a presentation I made to English teachers in another school and was able to report to him how much my audience, including the college professor who taught the teachers, loved his story. Even though Mickey was delighted by his success, he still had a minor tantrum every time he was required to develop his writing beyond the four or five lines he usually produced in a ten-minute freewriting exercise. At that time my class was located in a trailer, so I was able to send him outside to "cool off" and then join him for a talk. I told him that he must have a "sore toe" about writing because every time I asked him to do it he acted as if he were going to be hurt. He attributed the problem to me—I had impossible expectations—but then he laughed and, after a few minutes of kicking stones against the trailer, came back to work.

By the end of 1980–81 Mickey had begun to appreciate his own ability as a storyteller. A freewriting he titled "My Car" became the year's magnum opus. He spent considerable time revising this story of his Volkswagen "bug" and he did it with minimum resistance. After his freewriting, Mickey dictated supplementary information to me, discussed the way it needed to be reorganized, and revised it while I typed. Knowing that his story "Trees" was also going to be published in our class anthology gave him the incentive to change a confusing line in "Trees" that he had never before been willing to touch.

September 1981–April 1982

In September of 1981, Mickey was assigned to my class again, along with three other students—Cal, Gerry, and Jack, who had been in the same class as eleventh graders—and a fourth boy, Jon, who was new to my group, but not to the L.D. program.

Two of Mickey's first freewritings in September gave reasonably clear accounts of current events in his life and were more than three times the length of "Trees," his first freewriting of the previous year. The third piece, only eight lines long, began "Today I have been writing since first period . . ." (it was second period), but acknowledged that his writing was getting easier, somewhat enjoyable, and that even though it was sometimes hard, writing was helping him think of things "to do or say in writing." He had begun to use writing as a tool of thinking.

But that unfortunately was not the whole story. For Mickey and the other four students in the class, writing about ideas and information had been the most difficult writing task in the previous year. I felt it was important to begin the year with an activity that would help them master idea/information writing, since that is the kind of writing they are most often called upon to do in school. Ken Macrorie's "I-Search" paper (1980) seemed to fit this description. "I-Search" is Macrorie's alternative to the traditional research paper. The chief differences are that students choose topics they already know about and care about, use interviews as well as books as sources of information, and write informally. Macrorie believes this approach helps students develop good research techniques and write more interesting papers. I wanted to know whether the I-Search would allow students to use the skills they had developed in personal experience writing to write about ideas and information.

Theoretically, Mickey's I-Search topic, the Green Berets, was ideal for making the connection between personal and idea/information writing. Mickey had military people on both sides of his family and in his stepfather's family, so the topic was only one step removed from his personal experience. Also, he cared about the subject. He had been planning to make the Army a career and the research about the Green Berets was important to him. He did enlist in November, shortly after he turned seventeen, with his parents' permission and the understanding that he would begin basic training after graduation. One of the biggest problems in research—knowing what the questions are—ought to have been solved by Mickey's familiarity with the topic. Oddly, after he had developed the initial questions: "What are the steps to becoming a Green Beret?" and "What academic and personal qualifications do I need to become a Green Beret?" he had trouble asking follow-up questions.

Mickey had told me that one of the Green Berets' requirements was to learn a foreign language. And we had discussed the likelihood that this would be very hard for him. So it seemed natural to me to ask, "What happens if I fail one of the steps?" But Mickey didn't automatically think of that question. Also, he never had any doubt that the information he thought was true could be anything but true. From one source, he developed the view that Fort Benning, Georgia, was the only basic training center and had to be persuaded to ask the question, "Are there any alternatives to basic training at Fort Benning?" It turned out there were.

For the most part, Mickey seemed to enjoy the research, especially the interviews. The most difficult part of the research process was writing down the information he was gathering. My task, again, was to help him cope with the pain that writing caused him, but above all to keep him writing. This was particularly true as we moved through the stages of the writing process. I could not look to the other students in my 1981–82 Basic Skills class to support Mickey's writing. During the first term, when the students were gathering their information, the group was dominated by the negative attitude of Jon, the boy who was new to my class. He had been trying since the previous year to convince his mother to allow him to be placed out of the learning disabilities program. With my encouragement, he was "placed out," but he didn't actually leave my classroom until just before the students began their rough drafts. Cal and Gerry were no help either. Ensnarled as they were in personal crises related to being seniors, they never became committed to their I-Search papers. I had allowed the research time to drag on, hoping they would catch up with Mickey and Jack. They didn't. But all of us got very edgy. So it was with great trepidation I moved them into the writing process.

The journal I kept during that time illustrates not only Mickey's struggles, but my own tension as he moved through the writing tasks.

11/17/81

I have written "Rough Draft Due" on the board. This is it. We have to finish. Why did I let them take eight weeks on their research?!?

Mickey rereads what he has written, biting his pen tip, thinking. Then looks at his notes and writes again. I am writing too, trying to keep myself from being involved unless I am asked. Mickey has "gotten into" his I-Search on the Green Berets. He has skimmed old *Time* magazines, studied army recruitment materials, read Robin Moore's novel, *Green Beret*, and conducted two interviews. But I wonder if he's going to throw up his hands and say "forget the whole thing" now that he has to synthesize his information in writing. That's the way I feel whenever I get to that point in a research project. Mickey just looked up from his work—smiling!— and beckoned to me. He was using the brief outline I gave him yesterday. He wanted to know what I mean by "give an honest assessment of the academic and personal qualifications you bring to the Green Berets." I explained. He nodded, said "Oh, O.K.," and then *went back to work. He has already been writing for twenty minutes.*

Along with the outline, I gave him a pep talk about how good his information was. I also reminded him about his "sore toe" response to writing. I told him yesterday that he might have to write for short periods of time or tape it. This seems to have paid off. Knowing that he had permission to quit allowed him to go on. It reminds me of the way I behaved when I first started jogging. After I said, "I can always stop at the black mailbox five houses from the end of the block," I rarely had to quit before the mile was up.

After the students had completed their rough drafts, the next phase was revision. Students began this phase in "reading/writing" groups, listening to and criticizing each other's writing. The spirit was anything but supportive.

11/19/81

Mickey read his paper to the group today. I had told them to listen to each other as "uninformed readers," even though they had heard some of it before, so they would be able to tell each other what else the paper needed to say. Mickey was proud of his paper. But he covered up by reading first in the style of a third grader reading poetry and then, after I told him to be serious, with mock eloquence. Cal and Gerry were immature, even rude, during and after the reading. I wonder if they were jealous because neither of them has been caught up in his I-Search the way Mickey has been. Jack, who is usually very shy, made an aggressive statement, telling Mickey what he should have done. But they all gave good criticism. Gerry pointed out that Mickey hadn't started by saying what made him interested in the topic (that was a requirement). And Cal told him that "to help the oppressed get rid of the oppressor" didn't explain what the Green Beret does. Mickey's response was generally aggressive/defensive. Even when I joined the group, pointing out that he had written only the part of the I-Search outline labeled "What I found out," he said, "I'd say it does."

At the end of that entry in my journal, I wrote:

My goodness! They are so immature. How do I take myself seriously in that chaos? I'm looking forward to Thanksgiving break.

I was surprised to find that even though Mickey had denied, during the group session, that his paper was incomplete, the next version of his paper included all but one section that we had identified as missing.

The parts that Mickey did turn in needed a lot of work: clarification, development and organization. Knowing the kind of self-control he needed to rewrite those inadequate sections, I was cautious when I approached him about revision. I told him that if he included these sections as they were, they would detract from his paper. And continuing with my "acknowledge the problem" strategy, I suggested that he dictate these sections to me so he could concentrate on the ideas. I also pointed out that he could use one of his early freewritings for the section that was missing. He didn't take time to revise what he had dictated to me, but it was far clearer and livelier than the version he had handwritten the day before.

12/7/81

Today we worked on mechanical errors. Mickey made a huge fuss when he discovered how many there were, but he stayed after school to correct them. Even though he came in at 1:45 looking exhausted and fantasizing aloud about the chocolate cake he was going to eat when he got home, he fixed himself to the chair and didn't leave until 2:30 when I affirmed that he had corrected all the errors. There must have been thirty mistakes on two pages.

By this time I was worried that Mickey hadn't started a paper I knew he had been assigned for his government class. So I was relieved as well as surprised that he handed in his I-Search the very next day after he had corrected the mechanical errors.

12/8/81

Mickey turned in his I-Search today. He typed it himself. It's in a blue plastic cover with a white binding. It has style. The inside title is "What I Would Like to Do for Life." The first subheading is "In the Beginning." Some of the formal details and spelling are original. "Contuine from page 2" is typed at the top of page 3. "Contiune" is typed at the bottom of page 3. The major "What I found out" section was titled "The Job I What to Do for Life." I remember that we didn't discuss paragraphs in that section. There aren't any. The paper now has all of the sections that were missing from the rough draft, but no changes have been made to assist the uninformed reader. It is decidedly imperfect, yet written with enthusiasm and a strong voice.

In a narrative account of his conversation with an Army recruiter, Mickey has slipped in a telling bit of dialogue:

> He kept asking me over and over again if I really wanted to do this and I kept telling him, "Yes, I want to do this very much," and he said, "All right, we'll see about it."

In "The Job I What to Do for Life" section he wished:

> What I hope will happen is that I will get to the Green Berets and say "Look at me. I did what I wanted to do."

I told him, "It looks terrific!" Then I asked if I could put it away for a while so I could get some distance from it before I graded it. He was so pleased. I felt rotten for seeing all those mistakes.

Mickey had to go straight from completing his I-Search paper to working on his government paper. To my surprise, he didn't complain about it. But he did mention, with some concern, that if the rough draft of the government paper wasn't turned in on time (two days later), the teacher had told him to "forget the whole thing." The paper had been assigned at least two weeks before.

When Mickey began reading articles about the Defense Department budget that were incomprehensible to both of us, I suggested that he write about problems of the elderly instead. The White House Conference on the Elderly was in Washington at that time and I had cut out several articles, including one that discussed the economic conflicts between the needs of the young and the old. It seemed like a subject he could handle. Mickey was not enthusiastic about the topic and he did not understand the articles when he read them to himself, although he did understand them when I read them to him. I was pleased to note that he wrote summaries with commentary about each article with almost no complaint and promised to write his rough draft at home.

On the day that the government paper was due, I asked Mickey about the paper as soon as he came into the room.

12/11/81

Mickey slammed his books down on the table and shoved his hands into his pockets, shaking his head. His face was red. "I didn't do it. I'm mad at myself. But there was no way I could turn those notes into five typewritten or seven handwritten pages."

Nevertheless, with encouragement from me and the other students, Mickey began to write. He must have been waiting for me to insist because he didn't even have to leave the room to get his notes. I sat down at the other table to work on vocabulary with Gerry and Jack. I sat with my back to Mickey so I would be less susceptible to his struggle to write. After about ten minutes, something distracted me and I turned around. Mickey was standing at the end of the other table. His face was the color of his cotton jogging jacket—sand. His straight blond bangs matched the line of his closed lips. The untied drawstrings of his hood dangled as he leaned forward. Spread on the big table in front of him were more than a dozen jagged squares of paper. He was putting them together like a jigsaw puzzle. He is not good at jigsaw puzzles. It took me a moment to understand.

"The notes! You tore them? That's why you didn't write your rough draft? You tore the notes, but you saved the pieces?"

"I *just* tore them."

"You *just* tore them? Now? Why?"

"I was so mad at myself for not doing that paper."

"You were mad—so you tore up your notes?"

Gerry and Jack were staring in horrified disbelief. Gerry did not even say, "You creep!" I looked at the clock. There were still forty minutes left in the period. He said he had not thrown away any of the pieces. I started to help him put them together with Scotch tape. When I pulled off the tape, it stuck to itself or stuck two of my fingers together.

"This is ridiculous," I said. "Forget the notes. You know what's in the notes. Just write the paper."

"He won't accept it," Mickey replied. "He said, 'Five pages typed or seven pages handwritten or forget it.' "

"No teacher is going to give you a zero if you hand something in." (I was a little skeptical, but I said it with great assurance.) Gerry and Jack neither supported nor opposed what I was saying.

Mickey started to write and wrote until five minutes before the end of the period. Thirty-five minutes.

"It's only two pages and it sucks. He won't accept it."

I read it. "Write him a note. Tell him you know it's not long enough and it needs a lot of work, but you had a lot of trouble writing it."

He wrote the note, but I have no idea whether he handed in the draft.

I didn't see Mickey's government paper again until three and a half weeks later, January 6, 1982. He did hand in the rough draft and the teacher accepted it. Like everyone else's paper Mickey's rough draft was evaluated by a fellow student according to a set of guidelines prepared by the government teacher. They were designed to help students revise their papers using criteria by which the final draft would be graded: stating a thesis, supporting it with appropriate details, drawing reasonable conclusions, and using correct spelling, capitalization, and punctuation. But Mickey never did revise his writing and never wrote his final draft. I was out sick for a couple of days and then he was sick and when he came back he didn't have the government paper finished and said there was nothing he could do about it. I didn't check with his teacher to see if that was true. I did, in passing, ask him if he still had the draft of the paper he wrote the day he ripped up his notes. I explained I would like to use it for my research.

1/6/82

As I started down the hall at the end of sixth period, someone shouted, "Well, do you want it or what?"

Mickey banged his locker shut and handed me the rough draft of his government paper. Neatly stapled to the top was the dittoed evaluation sheet with check marks and comments by the student evaluator written in red Flair pen. One small section at the bottom included a "yes/no" column. Three of four checks on Mickey's paper were on the "no" side. Underneath the evaluation sheet was Mickey's cover, with "The old, by Mickey Richmond," one word to a line, slanting down from left to right. Near the bottom, matching his slant, was written in red Flair, one word to a line, "Poor Job at This Point."

While Mickey was avoiding writing his research paper for government, I had been avoiding grading those I-Search papers. I felt the final product didn't reflect the weeks we'd spent on the total process. After allowing them too much time on the research, I had rushed them through the whole revision process, rather than allowing breathing time between the rough draft, the revision, and the final writing. Finally I decided to grade the papers during the individual interviews I held with students about the I-Search process. In the discussion with Jack, the first student I interviewed, I came up with four criteria I used to evaluate not just the papers but the process: (1) the student's use of time; (2) the student's involvement in the process; (3) the student's efforts at revision; and (4) the student's final product. With these criteria, applied holistically rather than by assigning a particular number of points to each category, I was able to grade the students in a way I felt was appropriate considering their relative performance in that group. I still worried whether these grades would be appropriate for the "ideal" twelfth grader, who unfortunately exists only in my imagination.

My interview with Mickey took place on the day after he gave me his unfinished government paper. He was not ashamed of his I-Search paper. He thought people should be graded on "how hard they did it and then how well they did it. How well they've written it. The research job." Mickey thought he should get an *A* because "I had the hardest time out of the whole class to look for the stuff" and because "what I had to do was place it on a level where everybody can understand it . . . even you didn't know that much about it . . ." So he had to "make it on an elementary basic level . . ."

After putting me in that clearly inferior category, he hastened to soften the blow by saying of course he had grown up "with knowing a little more about it" because he had always asked his father and stepfather about the armed services. I teased him, suggesting that if the task was easier for him, he was actually defeating his case for an *A*, but he wasn't fooled or deflected from his evaluation, "I think I deserve an *A* and you do, too."

Reviewing

Mickey has come a long way in the year and a half that I have known him. Sometimes the journey has pained both of us. Back in January, at approximately the same time he was able to say to me about his I-Search paper, "I think I deserve an *A* and you do, too," he had said of the government paper he needed to revise, "Forget it, I'll take the *F*." But both the government and the I-Search papers represented growth in writing skill. In the I-Search, he was able to write coherently about how he had conducted his search, to synthesize information he had gained from various sources, and to reflect on what his future in the Green Berets would be like. Even though Mickey didn't revise his government research paper, what he wrote evidenced an ability to write in his own words about his reading and to relate these ideas to his personal experience. And he wrote for thirty-five minutes straight!

In that same government class for which he didn't write the paper, Mickey has become a star among students labeled "academically unsuccessful" because he knows and cares about the subject. His writing, as well as his talking, reveals an understanding of the subject. Recently, according to his government teacher, Mickey has been increasingly thorough in taking notes. He and all the other students in that class are allowed to use their notes in some short answer tests and all essay tests. His grades on most tests are good because they are graded for ideas, not for usage or mechanical features.

Now, in April, Mickey has already begun reading for a government report on the Supreme Court decision regarding draft card burning. The report is not due for two weeks. He has elected to deliver the report orally, an option offered by the teacher to all students.

Writing in my classroom still brings forth protests from Mickey, but he keeps the tantrums under wraps. He has made some efforts at composing on the typewriter and on the tape recorder and when he is pressured for time or when the subject is complex, he dictates to me. All of these methods seem to relieve some of his frustration.

During my Basic Skills class, Mickey is still frequently immature, but he has assumed leadership in helping the other students prepare for their government tests. I rely on his notes when the group plays a game for drill. As my student assistant during his free period, he is sociable, hardworking (either working on his homework or working for me) and *almost adult*.

Reading between the Lines

For an L.D. teacher or any other teacher who works with learning-disabled students, the question is always, "How differently do I have to treat this student? When a student can't do something that is a vital part of the curriculum and when that student feels very reluctant to try, how should I respond? Even if I can't always provide the situation that allows him or her to say, 'I deserve an *A*,' how can I assure that he or she will not choose 'I'll take the *F*?' How can I keep the student writing? And how can I keep the student developing his or her writing?"

Mickey's progress as a writer over the past two school years—especially his active involvement in the I-Search paper on the Green Berets and his failure to complete the research paper on the elderly—suggests some answers. I conducted individual interviews about the I-Search process with all my students. Because I was interested in figuring out why Mickey failed to complete the research paper, I continued to interview him. The subjects of these interviews were the research paper that didn't get done and an "ideal" research paper that would get done. Three themes emerged in these interviews: his need for control, his concern about time, and his great sensitivity to criticism.

Ken Macrorie (1980) has pointed out that rarely, except in school, are people called upon to "research" questions that the reader (the teacher) knows more about than the researcher does. Mickey's responses indicated how much knowing more about the topic than the teacher was, for him, a primary element of control. It was with pride and a sense of mastery that he told me:

> . . . my father knew about it, my stepfather knew about it. . . . You know what I had to do was place it on a level where everybody can understand it—even I can understand it a little better than saying "tch-tch-tch"—without, you know, writing it down and

> you not understanding what I said and then I understood what
> I write and we'd be meetin' at two different levels. I'd be on an
> upper level and you'd be on a lower level . . .

In retrospect, the topic for the research paper, problems of the elderly, did not afford him that same sense of mastery. When I asked him how he felt about it, he responded, "I just wanted to get it done for a report. I didn't really care that much about it at all." Asked to imagine a situation in which a research paper would get done, his first recommendation was that everyone should have a topic "they would enjoy doing, not something that someone else chooses for you."

Taping interviews or taping notes contributed further to his sense of control by allowing him to get his information straight. Interviews provided immediate feedback.

> It's better than reading it out of books—you can't ask a book
> a question! A book can't talk back to you and say, "This isn't
> right, you know, what you said."

Tapes also provided an accurate record: "I could understand what I said."

In contrast, reading and notetaking were a problem, regardless of the topic. He hadn't understood the articles on the elderly when he read them himself. He understood them "a little bit" when we read them together. But his notes on these articles were intelligible "for me but not for the report." Of his I-Search journals he said, "After a while you don't understand what you read. You write so fast that your mind's faster than your hand."

Certain requirements of the research paper seemed to contribute to Mickey's feelings that the project was beyond his control. His first response to my "tell me about the paper that you had to write for your government teacher" was a list of requirements for the paper with emphasis on the requirements that he could not meet.

> Well, that had to be five pages typed or with footnotes, quotations
> if you got it from somebody and quote the writer—that's kind
> of hard 'cause last year I never did such a thing . . . I didn't
> have footnotes. I didn't have the correct amount of papers. I
> didn't have my act together.

He was vociferous about the difficulty of writing a thesis before writing the paper. And even when it was suggested that it could be acceptable to write the thesis after the paper, he felt that writing a thesis "is the pits 'cause it hurts when you gotta do that. It gives you a headache and you gotta come back to it."

Recognizing the need for a paper to have a focus, he suggested that in the "ideal" paper, students should be directed to answer "who, what, when, where, why and how." Time was an important item for Mickey. In his "ideal paper" he allocated two weeks to gather the information, two weeks to get the paper done and then a week or a week and a half to submit it to a friend and then revise it. The total time was four and a half to five weeks. This was noteworthy because it was almost exactly the schedule his government teacher had followed. Yet of the time allotted to that paper he said: "I don't care how smart you are, I don't care how stupid you are or how average you are. There's no way you can get it done."

We had spent about eight weeks gathering information for the I-Search paper and then about six or seven days over a three-week period, which included the Thanksgiving holiday, writing, working in reading/writing groups, revising, and editing. Mickey was the only student who didn't think we had spent too much time.

Criticism was a sore point. Three weeks after Mickey received his rough draft with the student evaluator's criticism, his only response was to "see red."

> Just look at it. Tell me what I did wrong with it. How was I supposed to do it right? I don't feel like having someone tear it apart that I don't know. I don't think that's right. He just took my paper, read it, and marked over the paper. I didn't understand what he wrote. I can't read red ink that's squished all over.

He was not able to notice the positive comments that his critic had made—that he used details and that his conclusions were supported by his evidence. He also failed to note the absence of negative comments about capitalization and punctuation.

Mickey's sensitivity to criticism was apparently heightened by his agreement with it. Five days after our initial discussion of the paper on the elderly, when I asked him to read it again and evaluate it, he said: "I could have written a better job . . . I could do some spelling and punctuation and wordage . . . I didn't have a thesis; that's for sure."

Only with prodding from me did he venture: "It's in a rough draft stage. It's not bad." He put criticism of the ideal paper in the hands of a "friend" who would check the rough draft for "spelling, punctuation, all English stuff—proper wordage, sentences and all that stuff." When I pointed out to him that he had not made any provision about the friend's critical response to ideas, he added reluctantly, "Well, ask 'im to read it and to figure out what's wrong with it and what's mixed up, basically."

Reading/writing groups were as likely as individuals to be a threat to Mickey. Asked whether groups would be better than an individual critic, he launched into a tirade about people who "tear apart what you sweated into." (The tone of criticism in my own Basic Skills class this year may have been the basis for this judgment.) Then grudgingly he admitted the pragmatic value of the group: "to see if we had any more unanswered questions. So I guess it helped a little. But I figured I answered all of 'em."

It is interesting to note that even weeks after the I-Search paper was finished, Mickey continued to deny that there had been anything wrong with his rough draft. Yet he had, in fact, added the missing sections of the I-Search paper as a result of the group's response.

The need for control, concern about time, and sensitivity to criticism contributed to Mickey's writing and not writing. Control of the topic meant control of the language. "To help the oppressed get rid of the oppressor" (a phrase from the Green Beret paper) is a cliché and is uninformative. But it filled space on the paper and came rolling off his tongue and pen. Similar phrases might have been available to him if I had encouraged him to write about the Defense Department budget. (I had, after all, discouraged him from doing research on the Defense Department because I don't know that language.)

Control of the topic may also have been a bulwark against criticism. When the reading/writing group told him that parts of his I-Search paper were missing, he could readily reconstruct them. If he couldn't read his notes, he could write them from memory. One might imagine that the new information he gathered had become part of an existing verbal package. Control of the topic meant control of the connections between ideas. This facilitated the flow of language.

His knowledge of the subject also allowed him to ignore justifiable criticism about the I-Search paper. Although he added the missing sections, he never did explain what the Green Berets do or what their history is. But when he wrote about the Green Berets, he had no inner voice saying, "This is something you don't know—you'll never be able to fill all those pages." He did know. He didn't *write* all of it. But he *knew* it.

Mickey's concern about time seemed to be only partly connected to the pressure of real time and deadlines. He decided that the requirements for the research paper were insurmountable and so real time was almost irrelevant. In a similar fashion, the "no way you could get it done" (too much to do) feeling came not so much from the time allocated to the assignment as from the timing of it immediately after the I-Search paper, a major writing effort for Mickey. He had expressed a comparable feeling early in the year when he wrote, "Today I have been writing since first period" and it was second period.

When I, in my eagerness to help him get his research done, worked him quickly through the three articles that I had cut out about the elderly, I had in effect shot him out of a slingshot. On the other hand, the research process for the I-Search paper was long and slow. It allowed him to make false starts and meanderings that were close to, but off, the topic—a normal part of the research/writing task. During the information-gathering period, the leisurely schedule allowed time/space between each painful writing experience. But the most important ingredient in Mickey's sense of success about the I-Search paper was that he didn't just start in September of 1981. He started his search when he was a little boy, playing war in the trees.

Conclusions/Recommendations

These conditions helped Mickey to write and/or to develop his writing:

—He chose the topic for writing.

—He wrote freely and postponed concerns about spelling and mechanics until the end of the writing process.

—He taped notes, told stories orally, and dictated to someone.

—He used interviews to supplement information from books.

—He had an appreciative audience during the process of writing.

—He felt good about his rough draft.

—He expected to be "published."

—He was graded holistically for the process as well as the product so that the teacher's evaluation matched his own sense of effort.

—He was graded for ideas only, not spelling and mechanics on essay tests.

—His writing problem was acknowledged, and he was given a way to think about it, but requirements to write were not waived.

These conditions discouraged Mickey from writing or interfered with the development of his writing:

—He did not have time to "digest" an unfamiliar topic.

—He had major writing assignments following in quick succession.

—A great number of requirements were set down for an early draft.

—He received criticism, even valid criticism, that was heavily negative in tone, written in red, or delivered by a person whom he regarded as "not a friend."

Implications for teachers:

—We need to know the conditions that facilitate and discourage writing.

—We need to teach students how to give and receive criticism about writing.

—We need to learn how to deal with the defense strategies of our students and our own anxiety about their performance.

—We need to cooperate with each other when we teach handicapped students so that the total load of writing at one time is reasonable.

—We need to keep the working efforts of learning-disabled students so that students and teachers can see the progress made.

References

Macrorie, K. 1980. *Searching writing*. Rochelle Park, N. J.: Hayden Book Co.

A Teacher-Researcher Writes about Learning
Courtney Rogers

As a public high school English teacher who is committed to the teaching of writing, I have confronted week after week, year after year, the dilemma of time—there is never enough of it. It was with a selfish concern as well as with a genuine desire to learn about the writing process, then, that I began to investigate the effects of commenting on students' writing. If I discovered, as I suspected I would, that the comments I took hours to write were less than positive forces, I would have proved to myself something that the research and testimonials of numerous educators for years had failed to do.

It had always seemed to me that students who appeared already motivated to write and learn generally paid attention to my comments on their rough and final drafts and showed an interest in using them to revise their writing; students who were not already motivated when they came to my class did not show an interest in the comments but usually did show concern about the grade. Although it was frustrating to continue a practice that seemed pointless with these students, I could never justify to my own satisfaction treating their writing differently. So I continued to write comments about every student's drafts (after all, that was part of my job), but I began systematically to collect data on my students' views about this practice. Periodically I asked students to write about how they felt about themselves as writers, what they thought about their own writing, and how my comments affected their writing.

About two months into the research, I tried a couple of new strategies in my classroom to shift the focus away from my commenting on their writing and learning. First, I began to experiment with a technique discovered by another teacher-researcher, Marion MacLean ("Voices Within: The Audience Speaks," *English Journal* 72:62–66) of having students write comments about their own writing in the margins of their drafts. Second, after hearing Pat D'Arcy speak to my teacher-researcher class (November 17, 1982) on the importance of self-discovery in the learning process, I asked students to write about their own learning. Those in my four ninth-grade World Civilizations classes responded to a questionnaire that asked them to evaluate what they had learned from a Great Religions unit and how they had learned it. I taped discussions in which we talked about the observations they made about their learning processes.

I saw value in these activities for the students and for the research. As I continued to use this strategy in the classroom, my students revealed to themselves and to me some interesting things about what happens when they write and when they learn. I collected so much data from them, however, that the task of analyzing and writing about all of it seemed overwhelming, especially since I was still spending a lot of time writing comments about their writing! Finally, I decided to write about what I discovered from one set of data from one of my five classes.

> Writing this paper helped me understand the book better and helped me to get my own point of view clear in my head.

This was tenth grader Ann's written comment about writing her essay on *The Grapes of Wrath*. Her class of twenty-five students had

read, discussed, and written about Steinbeck's novel over the course
of several weeks. The culminating assignment was an essay. Students
handed in with their final product all other working drafts, from
exploratory to last, as well as a student evaluation sheet completed
by a classmate and a writing questionnnaire. The questionnaire asked
them to describe their own process of revision and to evaluate what
they believed they had accomplished in the writing of the essay,
considering the process as well as the end product.

Ann's comment was typical. Many of her classmates wrote about
new insight they gained on the particular aspect of the novel they
had chosen to write about.

Ray made a distinction between what he thought about and
understood when he read the novel and what he understood when
he wrote about it:

> I think that I realized and understood Ma's character more after
> writing my essay than I did when I read the book. I saw more
> clearly how Ma changed to lead the family after writing my
> composition.

Michele tried to articulate some of the feelings she had as she went
through what she viewed as an arduous, sometimes frustrating, process
that nevertheless led to something:

> I began writing down my basic ideas without any form. Then I
> tried to organize it a little, while trying not to look too much
> on the mechanical errors. . . . We got into groups and I was
> given lots of advice [from students] about what changes I should
> make. I tried so hard to get it all together but it just wouldn't
> fall into place. We got more suggestions and I was able to work
> with it more. Things were starting to take shape. . . . I didn't
> know how I'd make the deadline but I was very pleased and
> surprised with my final draft.

It was this process that provided Michele with a vehicle for learning:

> While doing this I really learned a lot more about the book and
> understood it better. Writing this helped me really look in and
> feel part of the book [and] also gave me pointers on how to
> write an essay.

Michele had struggled with reading the novel and with writing her
essay, and her comments made me suspect that writing about the
novel was what made her feel the reading of it had been personally
worthwhile.

For other students as well, understanding of their subject seemed
to improve as they began to control their own thoughts through the

writing. Suzanne and Amy seemed to recognize that it was in the actual process of writing that understanding came. Suzanne explained:

> As I wrote the timed writing, my ideas formed. Yes, I think I understood Steinbeck's ideas for comparison and I found my own.

Amy described her experience:

> Before I wrote my paper I had a faint idea on two qualities which Steinbeck had heavily stressed throughout the novel. As I revised (which I did a lot of) I became more aware of what Steinbeck was really trying to say.

Pam was dissatisfied, finally, with the quality of her end product, but stated:

> I did learn a lot about the reasons the author wrote the intercalary chapters. I also learned more about his purpose of writing the book in general.

For Pam and others, the process led to something worthwhile: the understanding of someone else's ideas, a good feeling about their final product, the clarification of their own point of view, or the development of new writing skills. The process for them became as important as the product, it seemed.

Kathy's comment shows that for her the process did not necessarily end with the teacher's grade on a "final" draft.

> I finally wrote the last draft and now re-reading it, I don't like it anymore and want to rewrite it.

Not every student saw value in the process. John stated:

> I don't really think that I accomplished that much because I was doing it only for a grade; however, I do feel that I did what was expected of me and to the best of my ability. I think I should get a *B*+.

Not only the process but his own product was of less importance than the grade. In his view, it seemed, accomplishing something worthwhile and receiving a grade were simply not connected.

When I asked students to write comments in the margins of their final drafts (at least one comment per paragraph), focusing on what they felt they had done effectively and what they still felt dissatisfied with, Marty complained, "It's a waste of time. I don't want to read it again. I didn't find anything wrong with it before, so why would I find anything wrong with it now?" Then, when I handed out and explained the writing questionnaire, she added, "We stay too long on the *same* subject; this is the *same* thing." Marty completed her writing questionnaire the same way she appeared to participate in the rest of the process: quickly and with little enthusiasm or effort.

Later, I examined what she had handed in: the student evaluation sheet completed by a partner was missing as were written comments of students in her revision group. There was scant evidence of actual revision in her writing. She described her revision process this way: "I just thought about what I was writing and wrote it," making changes in the following order: "from the beginning to make it sound right to the end, while changing the spelling or switching a few words around." While other students had filled close to a page in response to the last item of the questionnaire, Marty's complete evaluation of what she believed she had accomplished read: "I tried and learned to read over my writings before turning them in." I could well imagine what she meant by her response to the question, "What part of the writing process do you enjoy the most?" when she wrote: "Writing the end of it."

No wonder! For Marty, as for John, it appeared, the goal was to get it over with. They both seemed to be going through what they felt were meaningless motions for someone or something other than themselves in order to arrive at a necessary grade. It occurred to me that revising a piece of writing over and over conflicted with this goal on two counts. First, it prolonged getting it done; second, it implied there was something to be learned in the process that was not easily measured or neatly tabulated and recorded by the score-keeper, and there was the unmistakable insinuation that the writer was in some way responsible for his or her own process.

According to the questionnaire (and subsequent class discussions), the difference in comments and apparent attitudes between Marty and John on the one hand and Ann, Michele, Kathy, and their other classmates on the other was striking. The latter seemed to recognize, perhaps for the first time, that each possessed his or her own writing/ revision process. They were making discoveries about their own processes, abilities, and accomplishments by writing about them— discoveries they might not have made had they not been asked to think about the process they had used by writing about it.

Marty and John, on the other hand, were expressing a lack of sense of accomplishment, a lack of interest or faith in the process. There was not discovery but resignation alongside a plea for that acceptable grade.

I wondered why this difference existed, but mostly I felt frustrated because nothing I had done as a teacher had changed Marty's or

John's views of writing or of themselves as writers. Until I could crack the tough shell of their attitudes, I felt, I would be stymied in any efforts to help them improve their writing—and that I saw as *my* responsibility.

In an effort to make sense of their comments and my observations, I tried to diagram the characteristics of either group. Ann, Suzanne, Michele, Kathy, students who wrote about what they had learned with apparent interest and seriousness, demonstrated an awareness of and an interest in how they learn as well as what they learn. They were more process-oriented; the product was not all-important, but they took pride in it (Susan: "I'm proud of this paper"). These were the students who were interested in evaluating their own progress and appeared motivated to learn for themselves: they seemed to care about learning.

Marty and John did not appear to care about their own learning; they were writing for a grade, for someone or something other than themselves. They seemed product- rather than process-oriented, but lacked a sense of pride in the product. It was the grade, not the accomplishment, that mattered. Both students seemed satisfied with exerting a minimum amount of effort to get an acceptable grade. Neither displayed any interest in evaluating his or her own progress; that was viewed as the teacher's job. In fact, Marty and John seemed to view learning as something the teacher alone was in charge of and responsible for. Why would they want to write about a process of no interest or concern to themselves?

In spite of my sense that I now understood more clearly why these students had responded so differently to the questionnaire as well as to writing in general, I had to face the fact that my analysis of their attitudes and behavior was only a hypothesis. And how was that "hunch" going to have any concrete effect on my teaching or on Marty's and John's attitudes or performance? I still had to deal with them as well as strains of the same affliction in most of my students from time to time; few of them, after all, consistently exhibited full responsibility for their learning or faith in their ability to become good writers.

I had discovered no magic cure, but I began to see what had happened when students write willingly (or even in protest) about their writing processes, and, as a result, I saw for the first time something practical I could do about my frustration in the face of Marty's and John's attitude.

Writing about Steinbeck's novel helped Ann get her own point of view about his work clear in her head, but it was writing about her own writing that allowed her to see that this had occurred. As the process of writing about *The Grapes of Wrath* served to extend her learning about the novel, so the process of writing about the writing extended her learning about her writing process. In addition, writing about learning, I saw, had opened up a dialogue between my students and themselves and between my students and me that might be very important. That dialogue might never have occurred if the students had never articulated what was happening. If student and teacher remain focused only on the grade or on the end product of the process, I reasoned, neither will learn much from or about the process itself.

The written observations of all the students had served to clarify for me, as well as for them, their feelings, their attitudes, and their perceptions of themselves and their work that affect their writing and learning processes. And Marty's and John's perceptions of their own processes were every bit as important for them and me to know about as were those of Ann, Michele, Kathy, and the others.

At the very least, with Marty and John, this activity had put me, if not yet them, in touch with the fact that they didn't seem interested in learning for themselves. It had opened up the possibility for all of us to gain some insight into why this attitude existed, and with it, the potential for change. For all of the students, it was important to see how they had accomplished what they had done in order to consider whether there might be alternative approaches for the future (i.e., awareness precedes change). Wasn't it possible that if Marty and John continued to write about their learning, their increasing awareness of how they learn might generate interest in their own learning process and, in turn, a sense of that process as something they could control, something that mattered to them and for which they were responsible? At last I felt I had some practical measure for dealing with a problem that had always been too abstract and overwhelming for me to deal with.

Then it hit me. Marty and John weren't the only ones who seemed to feel that the teacher was responsible for evaluation of student performance and ultimately, performance as well; I had been assuming that responsibility myself. Hence, I felt guilty not only about poor student performance but about poor student attitude as well. I thought of all the ways I had for years subtly and not subtly reinforced students' notions that I was responsible for their success or failure, for their positive or negative attitudes toward writing and learning. The copious comments I had written on students' drafts and final products seemed to signify to some of them that I cared about what they wrote and whether or not their writing improved, but had it not also stamped my imprint heavily on what they had to say? Likewise, the grade most often came completely from the teacher and not from the student.

This time I had handled the grading and commenting somewhat differently. In asking them to assess their own processes and products, I had attempted to shift the responsibility for assessment partly to them. Also, by telling me what they felt they had accomplished, they were making me a more educated and informed evaluator of their work. As I responded on the questionnaire to their own evaluations, I felt much less discouraged while evaluating their writing because I was not focusing only on their final products; I was encouraged by what they told me they were learning in the process.

When my ninth-grade students responded to the same writing questionnaire after completing their essays on characters from *Romeo and Juliet*, their self-evaluations most frequently called attention to learning something about one or more of the following: the character who was the subject of the writing, the play itself, the use of constructive criticism, the revision process, and the essay process (many specifically cited organizing ideas, creating a thesis and supporting it, writing a conclusion, or incorporating quotes). In class discussions about their responses, most students indicated that they had learned something new about their own writing/revision processes as well. Recently I asked my tenth-grade students to respond to a questionnaire after completing a written assignment based on a career search. The last item asked: "What do you think of 'writing about learning' as you have done on this and other assignments once you have completed them?" Two students suggested that they would prefer a less structured format without teacher-directed guidelines for writing about learning. John and Marty wrote the following:

> *John:* I think that this helps me realize what I have accomplished.
> *Marty:* I think it's very helpful. It's better to write what you learn so you won't forget it. Also, as you are writing, you're learning about what you're writing.

I feel that many of my current students are accomplishing something probably few of my past students ever did: they are learning to analyze and assess their own growth, and they are acquiring an awareness of their own learning and writing processes that may make further growth possible.

As a teacher-researcher, I have come to see my role as a teacher differently. While my students made discoveries about themselves as learners by writing about learning, I made discoveries about myself as a teacher by writing about my students. I learned how important it is that the process of learning be one of discovery for us all. I learned that I can't do it all. I am still spending a lot of time writing comments on rough and final drafts; however, the final comments focus on process as well as evaluate product. Making writing about learning a regular part of learning seems to be heading both my students and myself in a more productive direction—toward a classroom where we all share the responsibility for learning.

Discovering Revision
Betsy Sanford

Kathy and I were outside at break enjoying the lovely spring day and each other's company. Kathy had brought her notebook, and as we sat and talked, she offered to read the poems she had been working on. One, "The Nose," was still in a preliminary stage. Another was about boats and was closer to being finished, Kathy felt. As I listened to all of the poems, I was struck by the variety of Kathy's topics and the sensitivity of her images.

"Kathy, how do you do it?" I asked.

"Well, I get all of my ideas poured onto a piece of paper, and then I get it straightened out," Kathy replied simply. She was articulating a theme I had seen repeated over and over in the previous few months—my fourth-grade students evaluating and revising their writing, quite willingly and with purpose. It hadn't always been that way. I had started out the year dissatisfied with the way I had always taught writing. Children in my classes rarely seemed to have the opportunity or inclination to produce "generations" of a piece of writing. They wrote stories, I read them and acknowledged them, and then they wrote more stories. I felt that I was the "keeper of the flame," that students were not working on their writing beyond the first draft, that they were involved only superficially with their writing.

Looking back, I wish I had recorded exactly what I thought happened in the ideal classroom where children regularly revised stories and produced final drafts. As clearly as I recall, I thought that a student wrote a piece, received reactions to his or her writing (perhaps from a reading/writing group or the teacher), and went on to write further drafts, until the piece was perfect in the writer's eyes and acceptable to the teacher. In my classroom, though, students always seemed unwilling and unable to revise their work to any extent. I felt frustrated by the demands of managing a program where, to my eyes, so many students needed so much help. I knew many teachers had successful programs, and I hoped that doing research on what I thought was revision might help me.

I began looking in earnest at the revision process in my classroom the day that I asked my students to write a short piece about someone and revise it. I gave them no opportunity to test out their writing on other students or me; they could seek help outside school, but otherwise they were on their own. When I looked at the first and second drafts I had collected, I tried to determine what my students already knew about revision. I'm not sure what I hoped for. I may have wanted first and second drafts that were quite different. Perhaps I wanted second drafts that showed a few thoughtful text changes, as well as more careful attention to capitalization, punctuation, and spelling. I think I probably wanted it all. I saw very few differences between the first and second drafts, and I concluded that my students couldn't revise effectively.

At this point, I began to think there was a body of revision skills I could teach my students, and I started planning how I would do it. I analyzed the errors in their work. There were all the usual problems: run-on sentences, overuse of some words, events out of sequence, too many "and thens." I presented lessons on these aspects of revision. At times the focus was on an isolated skill, and I lifted sentences from student work to illustrate its application. At other times we revised whole pieces together, arriving at decisions by consensus. One time in particular, a colleague from another school gave me three drafts of a piece of writing a former student had done, along with the questions his reading/writing group had asked. I showed my students the first draft, inquiring what questions they would ask the author. When I displayed the group's questions and the second draft, my class saw that their questions were similar and that the author had answered them. We compared the second draft to the third with the same result. In all of these activities my students were talking about revision, but I saw little application of the skills in their writing.

During this period, I continued to observe my students' writing behaviors and to make entries into my research log. I puzzled over what I was seeing, trying to decipher what might be going on during the writing process. I still didn't know how to get my students to the point that they could produce draft after draft, and I watched desperately, hoping something would tell me.

One day, during a health lesson, I gave my students a worksheet to complete. (It was sentence beginnings that they were to finish.) As the children worked, I noticed Cindi erasing. When I asked, she explained to me that she had thought of an addition to one of her responses. Just then, she had been erasing a now superfluous "and" and moving three words over to fill the gap it had left. It was a simple, logical explanation.

I found, later that evening, that Cindi was on my mind. I saw that her erasing and changing on the original paper had been revision, and I realized that revision of that nature occurs constantly. But, I asked myself, if it's revision when students write something and immediately change it, isn't it revision when the students, before they set their ideas on paper, somehow alter and refine what they are composing? I began to see that there was much more revision occurring than I had originally believed. I realized that I had assumed significant revision takes place only after the first draft is completed. Now I saw that my students were using revision skills I had not earlier recognized. It was about this time, I believe, that my perceptions about revision began to shift.

The following week, my students began writing personal experience stories. As they worked they tested their ideas on each other and on me. I saw students making choices and revising as they wrote, but perhaps I never would have known the extent of their choices if, almost by accident, I hadn't looked in detail at the progress of Cindi's story.

That morning, as students began writing, I observed Cindi as she wrote her first three lines, balled up the paper, and began again. I asked her what had happened. She explained that as she had begun her story, she had remembered something connected to the story beginning. She had decided to include it and so had started over. I was interested in her decision, and I asked her to let me know of others she made as she wrote. We agreed to tape an interview about the writing of the story as soon as she had completed the first draft.

Cindi sought my help throughout the course of writing her first draft. Both before and during the interview, she was able to elaborate on choices she had made in her writing. I began to see that there was complexity to the decisions my students were making, and that what appeared on the paper often gave little indication of the underlying deliberations. The class, including Cindi, began working on second drafts of the stories. Cindi continued to seek me out, asking my opinion and telling me of her decisions. By the time the second draft was finished, we had done three more interviews.

The drafts of Cindi's story and the taped interviews offer abundant evidence of revision. I wasn't surprised by that. However, at that point I was still expecting most revision to occur after the completion of a draft. I had a picture of students sitting with their drafts and thoughtfully making deletions, additions, and changes in word choice and sentence order, prior to writing the next drafts. I was unprepared for the extent to which Cindi had revised as she was writing.

Cindi's story is about a time she was bitten by a dog. Here is the entire text of her discarded first lead, and with it the first two paragraphs of the draft she designated her first draft. (I have made five punctuation corrections for clarity.)

> Discarded First Lead
> One day, I was outside around back, at the playground, with all my friends playing on the merry-go-round, *when all* [These two underlined words were erased on Cindi's paper].
>
> First Draft (first two paragraphs)
> One day, when I was six, I was around back, at the playground, with my brother, sister, and friends. We were playing on and taking turns on a tire swing when all of a sudden a white, fluffy, about medium size dog named "Snowball" came running around. We all jumped onto one thing, but we all fit. Snowball was jumping, barking, and running up and down a grass hill. Finally, he gave up and went home.
> After playing on the tire swing and slide, my brother and sister went home to do homework. We all went over to the merry-go-round. We could go real fast and see who could stay up the longest without sitting down. I never won. Then all of a sudden a black dog, medium size, chased people. Everybody jumped onto the merry-go-round but me. I ran, because I didn't know what to do. So I started to head for the merry-go-round, because I saw my friends on it. Before I could get on, the dog bit me. My leg was bleeding really bad.

In Cindi's initial start for the story, the setting had been the merry-go-round as the black dog appeared. By the time she had written three lines, her story had expanded, and she started over. The new version begins earlier, at the tire swing, with the appearance of the white dog. The story now includes Cindi's age and the presence of her brother and sister. This revision choice had changed the shape of the story.

I learned from Cindi, in our initial interview, of other decisions she made as she wrote the first draft. Two of them can be seen in the part of the text quoted above. Cindi volunteered that she had deliberated, in the second sentence, about whether to say "*the* tire swing" or "*a* tire swing." The difference, she noted, was "you don't

know what the playground looks like, and I did know what the
playground looks like, and I don't know which I should say." Later,
in the final sentence of the first paragraph, Cindi had debated about
saying that Snowball had given up and gone home:

> *Cindi:*   I didn't know how to say it . . . if I should write, "Finally
> he gave up," then write something else, or if I should just
> have left it, "He gave up and left."

Or . . .

> *Teacher:* How did you decide on "went home"?
> *Cindi:*   There's two ways that you can go to the playground, and
> he went one way, and it seemed like he was going home
> because we were in the back, so I just said, "went home."
> I wasn't sure if he just went out front to play or what.
> *Teacher:* So as a writer you're just making a guess about that? Are
> you saying that it's not worth your time to explain to the
> audience that you're not sure where he went?
> *Cindi:*   I didn't think it was that important.

Cindi went on to discuss other aspects of the first draft. She noted
the use twice of "all of a sudden" and explained, "I shouldn't have
used the same words." She planned to delete the earlier use of the
phrase, she said, because the second time was when the action of the
story really started. In another part of the story, Cindi pointed out
that "before I started this paragraph I went back to read the story,
and I saw that I hadn't said where the dog bit me. I said leg, but I
hadn't said where on my leg." Cindi noted that she planned to include
that information in her next draft, "because down here [she reads
from her draft]: 'I had to wear a bandage around my ankle.' "
Throughout the interview, Cindi continued to explain decisions she
had made as she had written. I remember realizing that the draft
alone gave little evidence of the amount of work she had done during
her writing.

The next step was to prove just as interesting and informative to
me. The day following our interview, I asked Cindi to look over her
first draft and write down any questions she thought her audience
might want answered. Cindi wrote and answered two questions:

1. *Q:* What thing did you jump onto?
   A: We jumped onto a wooden stand that had two sides to get
   up. One is chains, the other is bars.

2. *Q:* Where did the dog bite you on your leg?
   A: The dog bit me down by my ankle.

Then I asked Cindi to make her revisions on her first draft. Here are the only revisions she marked:

First Draft	Marked Revisions
were playing on and	taking turns on
	(deleted first *on*)
chased people	chased everybody
so I started to head for	after a while I headed for the
the merry-go-round	merry-go-round
bleeding really bad	bleeding badly
I still have a little scar	(deleted entire sentence)
that's very hard	
to see	

Cindi began writing her second draft.

When Cindi completed the new draft, I compared it to the revised first draft. I had assumed that after marking her revisions on the first draft, she would simply recopy for legibility. Instead, I was surprised to see there were differences between the revised first draft and the second draft. Some of the revisions centered on issues Cindi had already raised in the interview. For instance, her uncertainty about where Snowball went has been resolved: "Finally he gave up and went around front." Cindi has also eliminated the first "all of a sudden." There were other text changes that related to issues Cindi elaborated on in the interview. I concluded that the interview created an oral draft for Cindi.

However, there were also changes in the text that seem to have occurred during the writing of the second draft. These involved issues Cindi had not mentioned earlier. One of these can be seen in this excerpt from the texts. (Again, I have made slight corrections in mechanics.)

First Draft
   Jokingly the boy said, "What's the matter?" Kendra said, "Your dog bit her." Then he said, "Oh, I'm so sorry." He said that jokingly, too.

Second Draft
   The boy saw that I was crying and jokingly said, "What's the matter?" Kendra said, "Your dog bit her." He said, "I'm sorry." He said that jokingly, too.

Why, I asked Cindi, had she been unwilling to use "all of a sudden" twice in the early part of the story, but she had kept each "jokingly"? Cindi's response gives further evidence of the type of decision making she was involved in as she wrote:

> Cindi: Well, I have two things to say. When I had the two "all of a suddens," I didn't think that sounded good because up there at the first "all of a sudden," not too much action was there. But down here . . . that's when the story really started . . . I got bit. And when I said "jokingly," I like that because he *did* say "I'm sorry" jokingly. . . . I didn't think that the audience would know that he said that jokingly.

Cindi and I discussed other parts of the second draft. Looking at her revisions, I could see that some seemed to be products of our first interview. Others were revisions she had marked on the first draft. Still others first appear in the second draft. Eventually, Cindi and I exhausted the comments and questions we had about the story. Cindi was appreciative of the opportunity she had had to discuss her writing, and she was proud of the work she had done. I was appreciative of the fascinating process I had been able to witness.

In the next few months, the class continued to work on writing. I felt that I understood better the work my students were doing as they wrote, and I could see that a major result of my work with Cindi was my greater awareness that students were revising early in their writing. I believed I was seeing much evidence of this, and recently I discussed this with my students. In looking through their writing folders, I asked, could they locate any instances when they knew they had made a revision before the completion of a draft? I asked them to let me know if they did.

As I talked with my class, John raised his hand and stated, matter-of-factly, "I know that I never do that." I thanked him for his response, accepting what he said. A few minutes later, students began working on their writing. John came up to me. He did remember a place, he explained, where he had made an early revision. He had been working on a story about his grandparents one day, and halfway through, he had read his work to a few friends. One had suggested he substitute "there" for some of the "West Virginias," and he had liked the idea. He showed me his draft from that day, with the marks of revision on it.

The same afternoon, Matthew brought me a story he had written six months earlier—at a time when I had been convinced that my students couldn't revise. He explained about a plot change he had made near the end of a story:

> Matthew: I wrote all the first page, and then I came to the second page and wrote . . . ten lines. I kept thinking of other ideas, but . . . it was like my hand couldn't stop and it kept writing. . . . And so, all of a sudden I got it all clear what I wanted to write and I forced my hand not to write. . . . And then I got another piece of paper and I wrote down my other idea, and I read it over a couple of times. And so, I said, "That's the idea I wanted," on the other piece of scrap paper, and I put on the top "BEST." And so I threw away the [second page], and I started to write my idea and then more stuff came to me.

Other children came up to me that day. Kathy showed me where she had erased and reerased the ages of three children in a story, as she weighed the advantages of each choice to the plot. Stephanie explained the process she had gone through in writing the beginning of a story:

> And see, I had a whole paragraph that I had in my mind, that I thought was good, but then I stopped to think, "Well, this isn't what I really want," because I had a better idea. . . . I put a whole new paragraph down which I really thought was better than what I had planned before.

As these students discussed with me examples of early revision, another of my students, Rachel, gave me a chance to observe the process firsthand. I had just finished talking to a student when Rachel approached me for help with the story she was writing. It was a story about a playground accident she had witnessed the previous year. Rachel said, "I got stuck somewhere around [the third line] and went back and read it again." She had realized then that she should include that her classmate's fall was "off the monkey bars," and she added those words as she read the story to me. Now, twenty lines into the story, she needed help with another problem. She knew she wanted to incorporate the information that the principal had told the class they would be the first ones to know how the girl was, but Rachel wasn't sure where she should insert it. I suggested she write the sentence in the margin until she decided, so she wouldn't lose it. Rachel was satisfied and went back to her seat to continue writing. I was satisfied, too—my students had reconfirmed that they revise as they write.

I feel I have learned a great deal this year about how students write. At the same time, I think I've learned more about my own role in the classroom. I can see that as I worked with my students during the past several months, I gradually adopted certain strategies as a response to what I was learning. The strategies were spontaneous; I wasn't always aware of them or of the reasons that lay behind them.

As a way to gain understanding, though, I've tried to express those strategies as a set of guidelines for myself:

1. Ask students about their choices.

This year I frequently asked my students the reasons for the choices that they made. This gave me insight into the kinds of issues these writers were confronting, and I began to have a clearer sense of how to help them. I believe that my students began to pay more attention to their choices and to take their writing more seriously.

2. Be available to your students as they write.

I began to see that when students wrote, they frequently sought me out for help. They had questions about phrasing, or about the right words to use, or about where in a story to introduce an idea. I stopped scheduling small-group instruction or housekeeping tasks for myself during writing periods. Instead, I used that time to work with students who wanted help.

3. Allow students access to each other as they write.

For years, I insisted on very quiet classroom writing periods, believing that students couldn't concentrate on their writing if they talked. Now I see that as students discuss their writing, they are getting advice and resolving issues, and I am more comfortable with the inevitable hum.

4. Provide blocks of time for writing.

It is difficult for students to work on a piece of writing when they are interrupted. I try to schedule writing periods when there will be no interruptions, and when no students will be taken out of the room for special programs.

5. Let students know they will have the opportunity to revise.

I noticed, as I worked with students, that they asked, "Are we going to revise?" with increasing frequency. Some students began to approach their writing differently when they knew they would have the opportunity to revise. They seemed more willing to take risks, knowing they could later rework choices they felt hadn't been effective.

6. Look for evidence of revision at any stage.

Perhaps the greatest impact my work has had is my realization that revision occurs constantly. I now feel that my role is to find evidence of revision in my students' work. Then, as I talk to students about their choices, I can help them see the possibilities in their writing.

I'm pleased with what my class and I have accomplished, although I still have questions. I see less evidence of decision making in the work of my less able writers. Is there a difference in the process that these writers go through, or do they revise in the same way but revise less? Are they at a different stage of revision? Finding answers to these questions could help me as I help these writers.

I admire the work all my students do. As I watch, I see that they are writing thoughtfully, trying new strategies, finding out what works. Together, we are discovering revision.

Reading for Meaning: Trying to Get Past First Basal
Mary Schulman

The first-grade students had just read "The Hat" from their basal text, *Happy Morning*.

Teacher: What do you think the author did especially well in the story?

C: He did a good job on the pictures. I like how he made Buffy scratch his head so you know it's Buffy's hat.

J: I like how he made his hat in the grass and in the sign the same so you know it's Buffy hat.

M: I like how he made the bug jump out [of the hat].

Teacher: What are you still curious about? Would you ask the author anything?

K: I'd ask the author how the hat got there in the first place.
[group begins to respond to K's question]
Maybe the wind blew it there.
Maybe the grasshopper got in it and hopped away with it.
It could have slipped off Buffy's head and he didn't notice.

K: I'd ask the author where Buffy ran to and to tell what happened after he ran.

Teacher: I have a suggestion. I would suggest that the author make what he writes sound more like conversation. Instead of writing "The big hat! The big hat in the grass!" he could have written, "Oh—here's my hat!" and make Buffy react the way a real person would.

M: Yeah, he could say, "My hat!" . . . and use this mark [points
          to an exclamation point]. I forgot what it's called, but to
          show he's excited and glad he found his hat.
T: Yeah, and over here I think the author could put, "Yikes!
          A bug!"
L: Or—"Ahh! You scared me."
          [T and L point to the text "A big bug! A big bug in the
          hat!"]

These first graders' responses reflect those of experienced writers
and readers. As makers of language, they are not intimidated by
written language. They have made judgments as to topic, clarity,
completeness, order, and interest in their own writing. As they have
listened to or read stories, rhymes, poetry, information books, and
imaginative and factual books, they have formed similar judgments
about the writing of professional authors. These children perceive
themselves as readers and writers capable of using their knowledge
of language to question, respond, analyze, and evaluate written
language.

Using oral language to talk about written language was not new
to these children. In kindergarten, they had the opportunity to create
and read their own texts in a classroom environment that supported
reading and writing as complementary processes. As their kinder-
garten teacher, I encouraged and supported their attempts to experiment with writing. I responded to their writing and often questioned
them about things I wanted to know more about or that I didn't
understand. Modeling questions and responses as "Read what you
wrote," "Tell me more about . . . ," "This isn't clear to me—explain
what you mean," and "Does that make sense?" helped them think
about clarifying, adding to, and evaluating what they wrote.

Gradually many of the same questions and responses were utilized
by the children as they listened to each others' writings. A sense of
audience began to develop as some of the children anticipated
questions and responses. As they wrote and as they talked about their
writing they began to think about others' viewpoints. At the end of
Laura's story about fishing for croakers and eating them for breakfast,
she wrote, "Oh, I forgot to tell you, my name is Laura." After
Jennifer read her story to the class, someone asked her the name of
her cat, and she responded, "I should tell my cat's name 'cause some
people might not know."

Listening to books written by professional authors provided another
opportunity for the children to respond to and question written

language. In what I'll refer to as a literature conference, questioning went beyond who was in the the story and what happened when. As I began reading aloud to the children, I modeled my thinking process as a reader interacting with the story or text. Soon we began to work through it as a group. The children began summarizing what the story or text was about along the way, discussing things that were not clear to them, predicting what might come next, and using background knowledge and new information to form their own opinions and ideas.

First Grade

Late in the spring of last year, the opportunity to move to first grade with the children I'd taught in kindergarten arose. The chance to continue to watch these children develop and grow as writers and readers for another year was exciting. But I also faced a measure of anxiety with the decision to become their first-grade teacher. I realized I had to accept some additional unappealing responsibilities to the basal text program.

By the end of the first grade the children were expected to have read three preprimers and two primers in the basal text program. I was expected to administer periodic tests and record mastered and unmastered skills throughout the school year. How ironic, I thought. These children who had been writing and making meaning were expected to learn to read by reading a text that lacked meaningful content. Children made to read "Mack went up. Mack went up and up. Mack was up. Buffy went up. Buffy went up and up! Buffy went up to Mack!" acquire little incentive to read books on their own.

Just after school began in September, I enrolled in a course entitled "Teacher as a Researcher." During the first few weeks of this course, I began to wonder how many other classroom teachers felt similar frustrations and pressures when it came to teaching reading through the basal text program. Were they aware, as I was, of the shortcomings of the basal texts? How was I going to support my belief that children need a literature-rich environment as well as satisfy administrators and deal with the pressures of colleagues and parents to teach reading through the basal text program? These kindergartners were capable of writing more meaningful text and using more complex sentence patterns than the basal text. Asking them to read the same words repeatedly seemed to be an insult to their intelligence. When the children began to read the basal text, I did not want them to assume that any failure on their part to understand or make sense of the text meant something was wrong with them, but that the shortcomings resided in the reading matter. It was out of these frustrations and concerns that my research grew. My question became "What happens when young writers question and respond to the basal texts?"

The Study

A child takes great pleasure in learning to read some words. But the excitement fades when the texts the child must read force him or her to reread the same word endlessly. In the first preprimer of our basal series, a total of thirty-six vocabulary words were introduced to the children. These vocabulary words were frequently repeated throughout the text to form sentences of unpredictable and unnatural language as well as empty and confusing messages. In one story, the character finds an old wagon in the grass. It needs both a paint job and a new wheel. When the character spies the wagon upside down in the grass he responds, "Junk!"—a response that is far from natural for a young boy in that real situation and indeed far from predictable.

It's no wonder, according to Bruno Bettelheim (1981), that children are provoked to errors by the discrepancies between the way people ordinarily talk and the way characters are made to talk in the basal stories. A child may change a passage or substitute words that seem more sensible. Often a child's reading errors are a deliberate result of some of the pertinent thinking going on inside the child's head in an attempt to make the text "make sense."

Another sad commentary with regard to controlled vocabulary is that, when most children enter school, they already know 4,000 or more words. Even less verbal first graders have mastered well over 2,000 words (Bettelheim 1981). How many adults would be satisfied to read a book in which meaning was sacrificed for a limited number of vocabulary words? Unlike many children reading in the basal text program, if we become bored or disgusted with a book we can put it down or even throw it away.

By the fourth week of school, as I was expected to, I had formed three reading groups. Typically, they were divided into a high, an average, and a low group. Initial placement was determined by at least two of the following criteria: the recognition of basal text vocabulary, the results of a basal placement test, the outcome of an informal reading inventory, and a writing sample. Ten of the children fell into the "average" range. It was these ten children I chose for my research study group.

The time I scheduled to teach from the basal text was not more than two days per week, and the way I taught did not include using the questions in the teacher's manual. I began instead by using a reading conference quite similar to the writing conference and the literature conference that had been an integral part of my kinder-garten program. Prior to the actual reading conference, I met with the group to introduce new vocabulary in the basal story text and set the purpose for reading. The children read on their own and returned later in the morning or the next day to discuss the text. These reading conferences often began with the children telling what they liked about the basal story (what had happened). Next, they asked questions about what they were still curious about knowing or didn't understand. Finally, they asked questions of the basal author(s) and made suggestions.

The reading conferences provided an opportunity for children to apply some of the same evaluative standards to the basal texts that they applied to their own writing. It led the children to begin to predict and reflect on the story's content, to search for clarifications and elaborations, and to accept the responsibility for interpreting and constructing their own meaning. During one conference, Megan responded to a rabbit getting caught in a butterfly net, "I'd ask him [the author] how did Mack catch himself [in the net]?" The children spoke spontaneously and began predicting what might have happened.

"Maybe he slipped and the net fell over him."

"Or maybe he swung the net to catch the bee, missed, fell, and caught himself."

"I got one. It was early in the morning with wet grass, Mack slipped and fell as he swung at the bee."

It was Kevin who clarified and confirmed what actually happened in the story. "I think he just climbed in and just hid in the net. It says, 'Mack went in. Mack hid!' right here." (Kevin pointed to the text.)

These children actively and directly engaged themselves in problem solving. They selected, interpreted, and integrated information to construct meaning, even when the "model" (the basal text) fell short. They began to understand the connection between writing, reading, and language. Most often when the children explained what they liked about the basal story during the reading conference, they responded to the pictures.

"He did a good job on the pictures."

"I liked how he showed Mack was scared in this picture."

"I like how the author drew the bee chasing Mack."

I wasn't surprised. Embedded within the pictures was the real text. Bruno Bettelheim (1981) found, "classroom observations have demonstrated how children look at pictures, decide what the text must be, and then pay little or no attention to it." This may be why Megan and some of the children in the group failed to understand how it was that Mack ended up inside his own butterfly net. They read the picture, not the text. In an attempt to focus the children on the basal text, I photocopied the words without the pictures from the story "Friends," which follows.

> Friends
>
> Kim sat in the sun.
> Jack ran up.
> Jack was Kim's friend.
> And Kim was Jack's friend.
> Jack said, "Good morning, Kim."
> "Good morning, Jack," said Kim.
> Jack sat down.
> Kim got up.
> Kim ran up to the hill.
> Jack got up.
> Jack ran after Kim.
> The friends ran and ran in the morning sun.

When the children in the group received the three-page photocopy of the story, they were asked to read the text silently to themselves. When they finished I asked: "What would you say to the author about this story?"

K: The author really wasn't thinking about things. Sometimes they're in a hurry to get things done.

M: (pointed and read) "Kim ran up *to* the hill." It doesn't make sense. I think he should write, "Kim ran up the hill."

K: I wonder why did Kim get up when Jack sat down?

T: He was probably going to sit on her lap.

Krista attempted to excuse the author for his seemingly hurried efforts at getting done with his writing. The children, once again, tried to make sense of the text, but without the pictures to draw most of the meaning from, it was more difficult to make sense of the print.

Following our discussion of the text, the children were asked to draw their own pictures for the text. Most of the drawings were very simple. On the first page a girl was sitting and a boy was standing. The second page showed the boy sitting and the girl standing. The last page both children were running up a hill. One child added a ball in all the pictures she drew even though it was not mentioned in the text. When Kevin finished drawing his pictures I sat down beside him and asked, "Can you tell me more about your pictures?" He began with the first page.

K: Kim sat in the sun. Jack ran up. They're standing up and they're supposed to be friends. [turns the page] This is when Kim got up and Jack sat down. [turns the page] That's Kim in front and Jack running after her.

Teacher: Do you think it's a good story?

K: Yes, on account he made Jack and Kim friends.

Teacher: Could the author make the story better?

K: Yeah, add a little more pages. He could add more information about Jack and Kim. He could tell why Kim got up and Jack sat down. It's weird that Kim got up and Jack got down since they are friends. [turns the page] He could add more to page 7. He could change "Jack ran after Kim," to "Jack went after Kim up the hill." That's about it.

Teacher: Do you think you could write a better story than the author?

K: Yeah, with my own words.

It was unanimous. The entire group thought that they could write a better story. The writings in their draft booklets, as well as many of the suggestions they made to the basal author(s) during the reading conferences on ways to improve or clarify the text, confirmed my belief in their ability to make more meaningful print, too.

I decided to photocopy only the pictures from the "Friends" basal story this time. We briefly discussed the pictures before they began writing the text for the story. Three days later we met to share the writings. As they read them aloud, I realized that they had written their own basals. Surely the fact that they had already read the "Friends" text, I assumed, influenced the way they wrote. I tried again, but this time I chose to photocopy the pictures from a basal story they had not seen or read before. We discussed the pictures together briefly before they began writing. Four days later the group met to share their writings. The writing once again lacked depth and meaning. They had written another basal-like text.

The children and I both seemed convinced that they could write better stories than the basal authors. What happened? Why didn't they write the way they did when they wrote in their own booklets? I decided to tape record our reading conference the next day in hope of shedding some light on what had happened. I began with this question:

Teacher: Do you think you write better in your writing folder or on something like this (pictures from a basal story)?

T: [In the writing folder] because you have more pages . . . you can draw pictures . . . and you can write words that goes with the pictures.

K: I think I write better in my writing folder than this because of I get my ideas. I don't get his ideas because this is the book that *he* made and those [booklets in the writing folder] are the books that I made and I can get more . . . ideas from my books.

Teacher: Which is easier? Writing for this [the pictures from the basal] or in the books in your writing folder?

L: My books 'cause they make up the stories by yourself . . . This does . . . it shows what's going on in the picture . . . when you draw your own pictures you're telling yourself what you want to write about. In this [the basal] it makes the story up itself because what happens is it shows the pictures and it . . . the pictures really tell you what to write.

Teacher: And that makes it harder?

D: Yeah. It's easier in my books because in this book they make the pictures . . . and you want to do some different words and it won't go with the pictures. But in the books that we write, we make the pictures and we make the words go with them.

Conclusion

The children in this study have become active writers and readers intent on creating meaning. Their experiences as authors, choosing topics and evaluating their own writing, have pushed them to begin to read like authors. Reading and listening to literature have provided them with language models for writing. Responding to and questioning their own writing, each other's writing, and that of professional writers have developed their ability to make critical judgments. They view written language as something malleable, not fixed. These children have become aware of the choices they have and the strategies they can use as meaning-makers.

Implications for Teaching

1. Teachers need to create an environment and use activities that lead to valuable encounters with books.

2. Teachers need to demonstrate the pleasures of reading enthusiastically by reading aloud to children and providing opportunities for them to read materials of their own choosing.

3. Teachers need to model ways of choosing topics in writing and of questions and responses that will help children begin to make critical judgments about their writing.

4. Teachers need to model how to predict, question, and respond to literature when reading aloud to children.

5. Teachers need to help children refine their understanding of the connections between reading, writing, and language.

6. Publishers and educators need to view reading as a purposeful tool to learn about something meaningful while reading, not as an end in itself.

7. Teachers need to engage children directly and actively with the problems and shortcomings of the basal texts.

References

Bettelheim, Bruno, and Karen Zelan. 1981. *On learning to read*. New York: Knopf.
Early, Margaret, Elizabeth K. Cooper, and Nancy Santeusanio. 1983. *Happy morning*. New York: Harcourt Brace Jovanovich.

Early, Margaret, Elizabeth K. Cooper, and Nancy Santeusanio. 1983. *Sun up*. New York: Harcourt Brace Jovanovich.

What Happens When Eleventh- and Twelfth-Grade Students Do More than Sit and Listen? A Proposal for Classroom Research on Operative Learning

Ann Sevcik

Abstract

As a teacher of eleventh- and twelfth-grade psychology at Herndon High School in Fairfax County, Virginia, I propose to study the operative learning of sixteen- and seventeen-year-old students. I plan to investigate this learning process (operative thinking) and its products (operative knowledge) by documenting my students' performance on written and oral tasks, by observing their reactions during class, and by exploring their attitudes through interviews. I plan to generate and test hypotheses concerning the process and its products and to suggest teaching strategies that could facilitate the process and improve its products both qualitatively and quantitatively.

The methodology would be multifaceted classroom research rather than laboratory experimentation, so the findings would include detailed descriptions, hypotheses, correlations, and speculations rather than formal proofs of causes. The value of the proposed research lies in producing accurate descriptions, testable hypotheses, and effective teaching strategies using data taken in a natural classroom setting. In addition, the findings could provide a sound foundation from which to launch subsequent experimentation focusing on cause.

Definition of the Research Problem: Background and Research Questions

Operative thinking and its companion, declarative thinking, have been lucidly described by A. E. Lawson (1982). They are both learning processes humans use to acquire knowledge, but each process leads to a particular type of knowledge. Declarative knowledge consists of given (or declared) facts; operative knowledge involves understanding where the declarative knowledge comes from and what it means;

and it also involves the capacity to use, apply, transform, or recognize the relevance of the declarative knowledge in new situations. Operative knowledge is invented by working (or operating) on declarative knowledge by questioning, evaluating, predicting, or connecting pieces of it in novel ways. For that reason operative thinking is said to be procedural, whereas declarative thinking, internalizing declared facts, is said to be figurative. When students sit and listen to declarative knowledge, they can learn, but their acquired knowledge is limited and their learning tends to be prescribed. When students extend their learning to operative thinking, the situation changes.

My interest in operative thinking began with classroom observations in 1982, the first year I asked my psychology students to write laboratory reports on classroom activities concerning human interaction. I declared the labs' objectives and procedures, students gathered and described the results, and the declarative thinking in those three sections of their reports seemed to be clear, accurate, and energetic. They were supposed to continue their lab reports by using operative thinking to discuss (evaluate, question) the declarative knowledge given in the labs' objectives, procedures, and results, and they were supposed to complete their report by stating some insights or discoveries, that we called conclusions, derived by applying, transforming, or recognizing the relevance of the declarative knowledge. A few students did that, but most of them stopped after describing their results and turned in reports that had absolutely blank discussion sections and no conclusions. Others turned in reports with discussions and conclusions that were functionally blank. That is, the writers filled the last sections of their reports with restatements and summaries, but they did not evaluate, raise questions, or make predictions and novel, inventive connections using bits of declarative knowledge. They did not play "what if . . ." with the declarative knowledge they had available in the labs' objectives, procedures, and results, and so they did not produce insights and discoveries to serve as conclusions. All of my students were strong declarative thinkers; but very few of them seemed to be skillful operative thinkers.

My psychology students were clearly not thinking and learning the way scientists usually do, and that surprised me because operative learning is supposed to be a natural, spontaneously developed cognitive process (Piaget 1958; Lawson 1982). It is a process that is used effectively early in life, in language acquisition, for example, and continuously. Why seventy-five percent of my students, all academically successful and college bound, were not using operative thinking in my classroom baffled me. I puzzled over the problem and prodded my students, but for most of them that first year, their lab report discussions remained functionally blank at best.

The next year I assigned the labs and observed the same problem. Throughout that second year I made what turned out to be minor adjustments—they seemed to have negligible impact—and continued to puzzle over the problem. As my third year began, I no longer felt surprised when the problem occurred. I felt alarmed because the lack of operative learning among my high school students seemed to be pervasive, and in some cases, profound. That year in September, I decided to begin systematically observing my students. For seven months I kept a journal recording my observations and reflections, and from that journal a number of questions evolved. Some of the questions could be addressed by surveying the literature on operative thinking; some of the questions seemed to require further classroom research.

The Literature Survey Questions

Previous research on operative thinking helped clarify how the process and products of operative thinking can be defined and described. Just as Lawson's work helped clarify the operative process, the work of Holly Stadler (1984) helped clarify operative products. She suggested a conceptual model involving six types of insight: (1) associative insight, characterized by the simple combining of experiences; (2) aggregate insight, involving a range of experiential associations; (3) discrete process insight, involving a systematic series of actions directed toward some end; (4) ontogenetic process insight, focusing on the recognition of developmental, end-directed actions representative of a particular individual; (5) phylogenetic process insight; and (6) transcendent process insight. I found that those products could be identified in my students' oral and written learning, and that the model was also useful in helping them extend their thinking to higher levels. Therefore, in the proposed research, I would begin by using Stadler's model to define and describe my students' operative knowledge. I would continue to explore the literature for additional, perhaps superior, models, and I might also find it advisable to develop a model of my own.

The literature survey continued with my wondering what effect learning via operative thinking might have on the acquisition of content knowledge. Like many others who have tested operative learning, Burton Hancock (1984) concluded that it was effective because his insight-oriented (problem-solving) medical school class out-performed his lecture class on tests of content knowledge even though the measured insight skills were the same for both sections. An interesting tangent to the effect of operative learning on content knowledge was suggested by Audry Champagne (1983) who found that students' existing content knowledge tended to interfere with rather than enhance operative learning in elementary and high school science classes, and Robert Seigler (1983) found that students' content knowledge, both correct and incorrect, could create problems for operative learning in disciplines as disparate as physics and grammar. In general, previous research suggested that the effects and problems associated with learning content knowledge operatively rather than declaratively do not seem to vary across disciplines, and that in turn suggested that the process of operative thinking should be, in some way, common to all learners.

That observation gave rise to the question of whether or not the process of operative thinking has a neurophysical correlate. Nancy Lueers (1982) reviewed some evidence and concluded that support exists for the theory that two very different neurophysical processes— conscious versus unconscious learning—are used by the brain to acquire information. There is also support for her suggestion that a homeostatic balance between the two processes is maintained by learners, and that learners vary in the frequency and skill with which they use each process, with young learners relying more on the unconscious process and older learners relying more on the conscious process. The heuristic value of the dichotomy is supported, but its explanatory value seems to be insufficient. Another neurophysical theory suggests that operative learning might be understood in terms of brain hemisphericity. Philip Goldberg (1983) reviewed the latest brain research and found that theories concerning the functions of the right and left hemispheres also suggest neurophysical correlates for operative thinking, but while they offer more comprehensive explanations for how operative thinking works, the hemisphericity theories are also insufficient. Even though a broadly accepted explanatory theory is yet to be developed, the supporting evidence for these two dichotomies—conscious versus unconscious learning and brain hemisphericity—suggests a neurophysical correlate for operative learning, and that position can be supported further by the work of Daniel Alkon and Eric Kandel (Hall 1985), who are exploring learning at the cellular level as a chemical and electrical process. If the process of operative thinking is, as researchers suggest, a neurophysical process, then the probability of its being available to every student increases. Why it was not used by most of the students in my classroom became an even more baffling question.

The Classroom Research Questions

From this background of observing my students and surveying previous research, my own questions for classroom research evolved.

—How rare is operative learning among my high school students, and why do they think it is difficult?

—What happens when students' new operative knowledge conflicts with what they already know?

—Do students value their own insights as knowledge?

—What role does student expectation play in operative thinking? What role does teacher expectation play?

—Can operative thinking be taught?

When I considered focusing on one or another of these questions for this proposal, I found that I should not. The questions are convergent and need to be considered more or less simultaneously because testable hypotheses and teaching strategies could be constructed from them in a number of combinations. Taken together, my research questions could suggest answers to the study's primary question: What happens when eleventh- and twelfth-grade students do more than sit and listen?

Rationale

The problem I propose to study is apparently significant. Researchers have found that operative thinking is a critical cognitive skill in college-level work, and the reason it is important in college work is that it seems to be a critical cognitive skill in the real world, in every profession (Loacker 1984). Other researchers have observed that students arrive at the college level without this skill, and some have suggested that students' spontaneous, natural cognitive maturation is somehow arrested during high school or perhaps earlier (Arons 1984). My classroom observation over three years supports that suggestion, and my studies and experiences in learning theory underscore the significance of the problem.

But my proposed classroom research takes on added significance because the operative learning would be studied and the teaching strategies would be tested in a field study rather than in a laboratory. Behavioral research has been thoroughly and extensively criticized (Carlson 1984) for some of its experimentally manipulated results that, to compound the problem, have been drawn largely from subjects who are undergraduate college students. Critics argue that those results lack the validity of sound field research addressing the intrinsic complexities of learning in a realistic, interactive setting such as the one I propose to use.

Design: Procedure and Methods of Analysis

"Be careful not to hunt houseflies with a howitzer" is an old behavioral research caveat (McCall 1969), and it certainly applies to this study. Like houseflies, operative thinking can be so elusive a cognitive state that users find it difficult to focus their thoughts on it, but at the same time, it can seem rugged and automatic like innate behavior. Whether fragile and elusive or rugged and automatic, operative thinking and operative knowledge must, like houseflies, be stalked inconspicuously and quietly, captured deftly using appropriate instruments, and if possible, kept intact by sound documentation.

My procedure for this classroom research would be similar to that of a participant observer in ethnological research. In addition to the participant observer's advantages of familiarity and flexibility, my role in the classroom as a learner among learners and my placing special value on operative learning by focusing research rather than grades on it should produce two more advantages. My students' sense of self-confidence and independence should improve, and that in turn should strengthen and clarify their responses as subjects.

I would use the constant comparative method of analysis, and to promote reliable findings I would triangulate the data by observing the class, by interviewing groups and individuals using both closed and open formats, and by analyzing student writing samples. I would use analytic induction to generate accurate descriptions of operative thinking and operative knowledge, recognizing that it would not establish cause in any way. It could, however, help generate sound hypotheses, and like the constant comparative method, analytic induction would encourage reinspection and reinterpretation of old data as new data accumulates. As the objective of this research would be to generate hypotheses rather than explanatory theory, constant comparison and analytic induction are appropriate methods of analysis.

The subjects, one class of about twenty-five students, would not be randomly selected nor would they provide a balanced, stratified sample. They would, however, provide a realistic, interactive sample. If the group used for this research is similar to my psychology classes in previous years, more than ninety-five percent of the subjects would be college bound, about eighty percent would be female, eighty-five percent or more would be seventeen-year-old twelfth-grade students, and the rest would be eleventhgrade students. The subjects' expressive and transactional ability, both oral and written, would range widely from learning-disabled to advanced placement students; but their ability to think operatively should not be affected because the process is considered to be more maturational than developmental. For students whose written communication is limited, I would augment their data using individual or small-group interviews. The setting would be a large suburban high school with more than 2,000 students, ninth through twelfth grade. The research would take place in a traditional closed classroom, and my other four psychology classes would be used as additional frames of reference for testing the teaching strategies developed in the research class.

Documentation would include written, oral, and observational data. Written data would be collected using a variety of activities that I have tested and refined for three years and some would be designed as needed (see time schedule). I have learned that the variety and continuance of these opportunities to practice operative learning in writing seem to be essential. My classroom experiences, particularly those recorded in the third year journal, reinforced two basic learning principles: that the initial levels of operative thinking must match whatever levels the students can grasp, hence the variety, and that gently paced, insistent, repetitive help and guidance are required to elicit and reinforce operative responses, hence the continuance. Students must have many and different opportunities to make mistakes and profit from the resulting contradictions and inconsistencies if they are to become skillful, confident operative thinkers, and what is equally important, I must have many and different opportunities to respond to and encourage both the skillful and the reticent students. The primary written data would be drawn from the following.

A Lab Report Project: Ten Lab Reports, Two Memos, and a Final Report (1st Quarter)

I would gather baseline data on my students' operative thinking abilities in September by assigning a lab report with five sections: an

Time Schedule

	Data	Findings	Interviews	Teaching Strategies
1st Quarter	10 Human Interaction Labs 2 Memos Final Report Reading Research	How rare is OT (Operative Thinking)? What happens when OT leads to conflicts with what students already know? Do students value their own OT insights as knowledge?	V A L I D A T I O N	Strategies would be identified and tested.
2d Quarter	Psychobiology Lab Reports I-Search Project Reading Research	What happens when OT leads to conflicts with what students already know? What makes OT seem so difficult? Do students value their own OT insights as knowledge?	V A L I D A T I O N	Strategies would be identified and tested.
3d Quarter	Developmental Psychology Lab Reports Experiment Project Reading Research	What happens when OT leads to conflicts with what students already know? Do students value their own OT insights as knowledge? What roles do student and teacher expectations play in OT?	V A L I D A T I O N	Strategies would be identified and tested.
4th Quarter	Reading Research As needed to clarify and verify.	What makes OT seem so difficult? Can OT be taught?	As Needed	Decisions on tested strategies

objective and a procedure (given by me), results (gathered and described by the students), a discussion, and the conclusions. The first three sections would contain declarative knowledge while the last two should contain operative thinking and operative knowledge such as questions, predictions, connections, insights, and discoveries based on the declarative knowledge. Students who questioned, connected, predicted, and generated insights would be classified as operative thinkers and those who merely restated and summarized or who left the sections blank would be classified as nonoperative thinkers.

I would continue to assign the series of ten lab reports over six weeks to provide practice in questioning, connecting, predicting, and forming insights. After labs 5 and 10, students would write research memos reflecting on the operative knowledge they had developed already in their lab reports. The memos tend to encourage additional questions, connections, predictions, and insights, and at the end of the first quarter, the two memos would be combined into a final report emphasizing students' operative knowledge. They would identify their operative knowledge, describe it, analyze it, evaluate it, and compare its value to the value of declared knowledge. Writing research memos is a standard practice among professional scientists, and I have found that our lab project memos can introduce students to the kind of scientific thinking that goes beyond memorization of facts.

An I-Search Project (2d Quarter)

Students would conduct an I-Search (Macrorie 1980) on a topic they would discover and pursue through interactive writing and oral activities. The operative thinking in this data would be particularly useful in addressing the question of what happens when students' new operative knowledge conflicts with what they already know (e.g., about dreams, mental illness, stress, and so forth). Furthermore, I have observed that the operative thinking in I-Search projects tends to develop in a rudimentary, linear pattern of thinking rather than in a matrix or lattice pattern such as that described by Piaget (1958). Because of that characteristic, I-Search projects seem to serve as useful stepping-stones to more complex patterns of operative thinking such as those required in experimentation.

An Experimental Project (3d Quarter)

Students would conduct formal experiments with predictive hypotheses and independent and dependent variables, and they would write reports similar to but more extensive and complex than a lab report. The experiment would provide an opportunity to use lattice-type operative thinking, and it would also provide an opportunity for students to formulate insights that challenge what they believe to be true—in this case, the hypotheses they used for their experiments.

Reading Research (1st, 2d, 3d, and 4th Quarters)

As they read each chapter in their psychology textbooks, students would gather data on their own reading, studying, and test-taking behaviors. During the first quarter they would write journals about preparing for and taking the objective reading comprehension tests on four chapters, and they would keep a frequency polygon on their test scores and a bar graph on the types of errors they made. During the second quarter, I would require that they use several reading and studying strategies that should increase their test scores. Through four more chapters they would keep their charts and journals, recording their reactions to the new strategies, and at the end of the quarter, they would analyze their data. Their data would be declarative knowledge, and they would analyze it, identifying behaviors that they feel had influenced both their test scores and their attitudes toward reading and studying. They would then use operative thinking to isolate the helpful behaviors and arrange them into a reading/studying plan to be tested during the third quarter. The cycle would be repeated during the third quarter; students would gather declarative knowledge about their own reading, studying, and test taking, and then they would reflect upon it operatively to produce insights they could test through the fourth quarter.

The interview data for this proposed research would be gathered through large and small class discussions, usually related to the operative process and products in students' writing and to the interaction activities related to their writing, such as peer reviews. Whenever possible, the discussions would be tape-recorded, but some of the interviews would be done at appropriate informal moments, so I would also keep that data in the interview log.

I would record the written, oral, and observational data as field notes, and I would reflect upon them frequently, at least once a week, as I did in the journal that led to my research questions. I would keep the data in separate folders rather than in bound notebooks because that would provide the flexibility required in continuous comparative analysis, and it would also make it practical to produce, as needed, periodic memos on my findings.

Value of the Study

When "back to basics" is emphasized, as it is currently, the educational community is essentially choosing to emphasize declarative rather than operative thinking. It is choosing to emphasize the sit-and-listen approach to learning. That can be essential learning, but it is only half of what is needed to encourage the complete cognitive maturation and development of our young people.

What has happened as a result of long-term emphasis on declarative thinking was considered by Arnold Arons in his research on operative thinking using tests that focused on arithmetical reasoning with ratios and on awareness of the necessity of controlling variables in deducing cause-effect relationships in experiments. His research led to a disturbing conclusion.

> [High school students] acquire no experience of what understanding really entails. They cannot test their "knowledge" for plausible consequences or for internal consistency; they have no sense of where accepted ideas or results come from, how they are validated, or why they are to be accepted or believed. Students acquire the notion that knowledge resides in memorized assertions, esoteric technical terminology, and regurgitation of received "facts."
>
> This educational failure is by no means confined to the sciences. It pervades our entire system, being equally manifest in the social sciences and humanities (Arons 1984, 213).

And the problem is by no means a new one. In *The Aims of Education*, Alfred North Whitehead (1929) warned us to beware of "inert ideas" that are taken into the mind without being tested or utilized. We still seem to have a galloping case of that problem, and my proposed research could provide two ways to address it: a clearer understanding by educational researchers of what happens when students use operative learning in a natural classroom setting and a clearer understanding by teachers of what they could do to facilitate it.

References

Arons, A. B. 1984. Education through science. *Journal of College Science Teaching* 13 (4): 210–20.

Carlson, R. 1985. Research foul-ups and blunders. *Science News* 127 (8): 120.

Champagne, A. B., R. F. Gunstone, and L. E. Klopfer. 1983. Naive knowledge and science learning. *Research in Science and Technological Education* 1:173–83.

Goldberg, P. 1983. *The intuitive edge: Understanding and developing intuition.* New York: Tarcher Press.

Hall, S. S. 1985. Aplysia and hermissenda: Two snails are leading the race to trace the molecules of memory. *Science 85* 6 (4): 31–39.

Hancock, B. W., W. C. Coscarelli, and G. P. White. 1983. Critical thinking and content acquisition using a modified guided design process for large course sections. *Educational and Psychological Research* 3:139–49.

Lawson, A. E. 1982. The reality of general cognitive operations. *Science Education* 66:229.

Loacker, G., L. Cromwell, J. Feb, and D. Rutherford. 1984. *Analysis and communication at Alverno: An approach to critical thinking.* Milwaukee, Wis.: Alverno Productions.

Lueers, N. M. 1982. Learning and acquisition—How real is the dichotomy: Some neurological evidence. Paper presented at the Annual Conference of Teachers of English to Speakers of Other Languages, Honolulu, Hawaii, May.

Macrorie, K. 1980. *Searching writing.* Rochelle Park, N.J.: Hayden.

McCall, G. J., and J. L. Simmons. 1969. *Issues in participant observation.* Reading, Mass.: Addison-Wesley.

Piaget, J., and B. Inhelder. 1958. *Growth of logical thinking.* New York: Basic Books.

Seigler, R. S. 1983. How knowledge influences learning. *American Scientist* 71:631–38.

Stadler, H. 1984. Types of insight. *American Mental Health Counselors Association Journal* 6:20–29.

Whitehead, A. N. 1929. *The aims of education.* New York: Macmillan.

Appendix A
Sample Course Outline

English/Education 696

September 13

Topic for discussion: Introduction to the course, research questions
Refreshments: ——————— & ———————

September 27

Assignment prepared: In research log, write an observation of students
writing and a reflection on the observation.

Topic for discussion: The history of writing research and methodology

Articles for discussion:	Discussion leaders:
Eisner, "Can Educational Research Inform Educational Practice?"	———————
Graves, "A New Look at Writing Research"	———————
Graves, "Where Have All the Teachers Gone?"	———————

Refreshments: ——————— & ———————

October 11

Assignment prepared: Find out something about what your students
think about your research question; document, continue log.

Topic for discussion: The teacher as researcher

Articles for discussion:	Discussion leaders:
Goswami, "Teachers as Researchers"	———————
Mohr, "The Teacher as Researcher"	———————

Perl, "Research as Discovery"   _____

Refreshments: _____ & _____

October 25

Assignment prepared: Plan what kinds of data you will collect, continue log, begin collecting data.

Topic for discussion: Classroom research methods

Articles for discussion: Discussion leaders:

Graves, "Writing Research for the Eighties"   _____

Kantor and Nelson, "Context-Dependent Studies"   _____

Hoagland, "On Becoming a Teacher-Researcher"   _____

Speaker: Nancy Hoagland

Refreshments: _____ & _____

November 8

Assignment prepared: Collect more data; continue log.

Topic for discussion: Relationships between theory and research

Articles for discussion: Discussion leaders:

Emig, "Non-Magical Thinking"   _____

Heath, "The Functions and Uses of Literacy"   _____

Moffett, "Reading and Writing as Meditation"   _____

Refreshments: _____ & _____

November 29

Assignment prepared: Continue data collection; write about your research question.

Topic for discussion: The research process

Articles for discussion: Discussion leaders:

Stallard, "An Analysis of the Writing Behavior of Good Student Writers"   _____

Stallard, "The Composing Processes of Upper-Level College Students"   _____

Moran, "Teaching Writing/Teaching Literature"

MacLean, "Voices Within: The Audience
Speaks"

Refreshments: _____ & _____

December 13

Assignment prepared: Finish data collection.

Topic for discussion: Data analysis

Articles for discussion: Discussion leaders:
Giacobbe, "Kids Can Write the First Week of
School"
Lofland and Lofland, "Analyzing Data"

Refreshments: _____ & _____

January 3

Assignment prepared: Review log and data, allow separation, achieve
distance.

Topic for discussion: Data analysis, model studies

Articles for discussion: Discussion leaders:
Estabrook, "Talking about Writing"
Kamler, "One Child, One Teacher, One Class-
room"
Womble, "Process and Processor"

In class: Writing and read-around: What is your question now and
what are your tentative findings?

Refreshments: _____ & _____

January 17

Assignment prepared: Write an exploratory draft.

Topic for discussion: Data analysis and writing

Speaker: Marie Wilson Nelson

In class: Discussion and support group meetings, reading and discussion of exploratory drafts.

Refreshments: _____ & _____

February 7

Assignment prepared: Create a visual representation of your data (chart, diagram, map, etc.).

Topic for discussion: Picturing data

Guest speakers: Teacher-researchers from previous seminars

In class: Discuss and exchange visual representations

Refreshments: _____ & _____

February 28

Assignment prepared: Draft #1

In class: Group meetings, reading and discussion of drafts.

Refreshments: _____ & _____

March 14

Assignment prepared: Revision of draft #1

Topic for discussion: Writing about research

Articles for discussion: Discussion leaders:
Murray, "Write Research to Be Read"   _____
Graves, "Sixty Minutes I and II"   _____

In class: Support groups meet to discuss revision of drafts.

Refreshments: _____ & _____

April 4

Assignment prepared: Draft #2

In class: Group meetings, reading and discussion of drafts.

Refreshments: _____ & _____

April 18

Assignment prepared: Prepare a ten-minute presentation on research, describing search and findings.

Refreshments: _____ & _____

April 25

Assignment prepared: Final draft of article for publication.

In class: Continue ten-minute presentations on research.

Refreshments: _____ & _____

May 16

Publication dinner meeting.

Appendix B
Sample Course Description

Research in Writing: A Teacher-Researcher Seminar (English/ Education 696) Northern Virginia Writing Project, George Mason University

The purpose of this course is to acquaint teachers with research in writing and its methods and to support them as they prepare and conduct research studies in their classrooms. The text for the course is a series of articles from the GMU Writing Research Center resource file. The articles will be copied for a reasonable fee.

The four assignments of the course are the following:

1. A research log consisting of a series of entries to include observations in the classroom, reflections on the observations, refining of research questions, collections and comparisons of data, and documentation of the role of the teacher-researcher. In order for the instructor to assist in the research process, each teacher will turn in at each class meeting copies of the latest work he or she is doing on the research project, commenting in a folder provided for the purpose. The folder will be returned at the next class meeting with the instructor's comments added.

2. A class discussion on one or more of the articles of the text.

3. Either a research proposal, an I-Search paper (after Ken Macrorie), or an article about research findings. The choice of final draft will be made during the course in consultation with the instructor.

4. A ten-minute report of the research findings and proposals that are presented in [emerge from] the writing of assignment 3. These will be given to the other class members during the final sessions of the course.

Both the writing and the report are meant to be in a form that communicates to other teachers and offers them helpful information about the teaching of writing.

Class sessions will usually be divided. One half of the meeting will include either discussions of assigned articles or presentations by guests who will discuss their own research with the class. The second half of the meeting will be a discussion in small research support groups to which each teacher-researcher belongs. There, members will read and discuss log entries and give each other suggestions about the research, serving as sounding boards for the researchers' developing ideas and theories. The group will also help each other analyze and validate data.

Teachers may decide to conclude the course with a publication dinner party. After the course the teacher-researchers will become a part of an informal network and will be encouraged to publish their findings in professional journals and ERIC, to apply for NCTE Teacher-Researcher grants, and to give presentations based on their findings.

Appendix C
Sample Research Proposal Outline

1. Abstract—brief summary of proposal.
2. Definition of research problem—research questions, objectives, your interest in problem, your background in relation to questions.
3. Rationale—description of significance of your study, related research, why do it?
4. Plans for study—design and procedure, setting, subjects, instruments, data to be collected, method of data analysis.
5. Work plan—time schedule.
6. Value of study—intended audience, impact of research, dissemination plans.
7. References.

Authors

Marian M. Mohr is an English and resource teacher in the Fairfax County Public Schools, Fairfax, Virginia, and Co-director of the Northern Virginia Writing Project at George Mason University, also in Fairfax, Virginia. She is the author of *Revision: The Rhythm of Meaning*, a book for teachers of writing.

Marion S. MacLean is an English and resource teacher in the Fairfax County Public Schools. She is a member of the Northern Virginia Writing Project, a Ph.D. candidate at New York University, and author of "Voices Within: The Audience Speaks."